SUPER FOODS
FOR SUPER KIDS
COOKBOOK

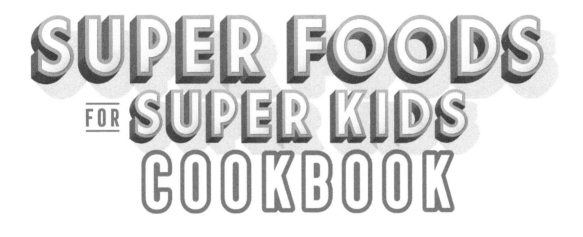

SUPER FOODS
FOR SUPER KIDS
COOKBOOK

50 delicious (and secretly healthy)
recipes kids will love to make

NOELLE MARTIN, MScFN, RD

PHOTOGRAPHY BY JOHNNY AUTRY
ILLUSTRATIONS BY RODRIGO CORDEIRO

ROCKRIDGE
PRESS

Interior and Cover Designer: Linda Snorina
Art Producer: Maura Boland
Editor: Lauren Ladoceour
Production Editor: Mia Moran
Photography © 2019 Johnny Autry. Food styling by Charlotte Autry.
Illustration © 2019 Rodrigo Cordeiro

ISBN: Print 978-1-64152-900-6 | eBook 978-1-64152-901-3

R0

To my mom, husband,
and sons Clay, Wes, and Rhett,
who made me a mama
and are the
best Super Chefs
I could ask for.

CONTENTS

CALLING ALL SUPER KIDS

ARE YOU READY TO MAKE FUN AND DELICIOUS FOOD?

Then you've come to the right place! This cookbook is full of recipes that YOU can make and eat at home, school, and even on the way to team practice. That's right: You are going to be a superhero in the kitchen, and your new secret identity is Super Chef. Every superhero has a mission, special gear, headquarters, and a sidekick. Here are yours:

YOUR MISSION: Choose foods that fuel your body with good energy to play, learn, and grow.

YOUR GEAR: Recipes listing the ingredients and kitchen tools you need and the steps to make food.

YOUR HEADQUARTERS: The kitchen.

YOUR SIDEKICK: Some recipes have steps that are best to do with an adult present. If you see a 🖐, that is the signal to grab your parent or another grown-up to be with you for that step. Don't feel badly about asking for an extra hand. Even the greatest of superheroes need a sidekick to help save the day.

Before we head into this crusade, let me assure you that many of the things you already love are in this cookbook. There are recipes for smoothies, muffins, eggs, and even brownies. Some recipes might have new foods or things you're still learning to like. That's okay! It adds to the adventure. Super Chefs, are you ready? Let's get cooking!

A NOTE TO GROWN-UPS

When kids have the opportunity to prepare food in the kitchen, they develop a sense of autonomy and adventure that goes far beyond sitting down to a meal that was prepared for them. Children are more likely to try new foods when they have exposure to them outside of mealtimes. They're also less likely to complain if they've helped prepare the recipes.

This book is written for kids 8 to 12 years of age. The information and recipes focus on the power that food has in keeping us healthy, and encourages children to eat more whole foods and fewer processed ones. It is also designed to increase kids' knowledge and comfort level in the kitchen. Simple tasks such as finding ingredients and measuring, as well as more advanced ones such as chopping vegetables and using the stove or oven are taught with clear directions. You'll also find fun nutrition lessons for kids throughout—all meant to inspire them for a lifetime of healthy eating. (For the adults, we've included more detailed nutritional content for each recipe in the back of the book, in case you're wondering about the sugar, fat, or protein in each dish.) There are also allergen labels to help with ingredient awareness and safety. You can support the Super Chef in your life by reading through the recipes with them, offering to take them to the grocery store, and being available for questions and help as needed.

Chances are good that your child will want to make all the recipes right away. Kids are amazing that way—they just want to go for it!

To help keep things realistic, have your child get a pen and paper before you open the book and make a plan for when you can cook a few of the recipes over the coming week or month, and then set a time to look through the book again to find new ones. Making this a routine will keep them interested and excited over time.

The recipes in this book are amazing conversation starters. You can chat with your child about the taste and texture of foods before and after cooking, the nutritional power of some star ingredients, and what it means to nourish our bodies well.

Many of the steps can be safely completed by 8- to 12-year-olds; however, every child is different in their experience, skills, and abilities. The recipes have a note at the top and a ✋ anytime that a knife, stove, or oven is needed. It is also noted if measuring is part of the recipe directions. These four basic skills are described in detail for our Super Chefs in chapter 2, but you may want to ask your child to include you in these steps until you both feel confident that they can complete the tasks independently.

Overall, I hope this book provides hours of fun in the kitchen for you and your children, and that while preparing and eating these recipes, your child gets excited about making healthy choices, develops a positive relationship with food, and takes ownership in helping to nourish themselves and others.

GETTING STARTED

Our story starts in the kitchen. You're no stranger to its pots and pans, goodies in the pantry, and fridge full of groceries. Now's your chance to learn to make the most of everything inside so you can start cooking like a true Super Chef.

SUPER FOODS

Food is powerful, and some of your favorite meals and ingredients come loaded with all sorts of good things to make you feel like a superhero.

WHERE HEROES GET THEIR POWERS

Have you ever wondered how your muscles and bones grow? Or how you have the energy to run, and learn, and play? It's all from the foods we eat!

What can we do to make sure we get all the superpowers that food offers? Use healthy eating habits, just like your favorite superheroes do.

Whole foods will always save the day. Foods that pack the most power are often ones that don't come in a package: Think oats, almonds, and apples. They usually live around the edges of a grocery store (not in the middle rows).

Beware of hidden ingredients. Some foods have a lot of added sugar and color. Use your superhero skills to read the ingredient list and know what you are putting into your body.

Pack a powerful punch of nutrition. Baking muffins? Add spinach to the batter and pumpkin seed butter as a topping. These foods add iron and protein for your mighty muscles to grow.

Be a social super star. Enjoy making and eating meals with your family and friends.

Super Foods' Secret Identities

There are so many ingredients to choose from that are packed with nutrition and flavor. We will explore many of them in the recipes of this book. Here are a few really powerful ones and examples of the types of recipes you can make with each one. Which one are you most excited to eat?

SUPER FOOD	WHAT IT IS	THE GOOD STUFF	TASTY TREAT
AVOCADO	Fruit	Energy-, brain-, and blood-building minerals	Dips, brownies, and smoothies
BLACK BEANS	Legume	Protein to support growth and fiber	Tacos, salads, and cookies
BROCCOLI	Vegetable	Bone-building minerals and antioxidants to fight sickness	Stir-fries, salads, and fritters
GRAPES	Fruit	Heart-healthy antioxidants	Snacks and salads
KALE	Vegetable	Vitamins, minerals, and antioxidants	Smoothies, sauces, and chips
LENTILS	Legume	Protein to support growth and fiber	Salads, muffins, and curries
PEAS	Legume	Protein, vitamins, and minerals to support growth; fiber to keep things moving through our intestines	Pasta dishes, brownies, and with rice
TOMATOES	Fruit	Vitamin C to fight off a cold and antioxidants to fight off cancer	Salads, sauces, and wraps
WALNUTS	Nut	Brain- and eye-building omega-3 fatty acids	Cookies, granola, and muffins

RULES TO READ BEFORE SPRINGING INTO ACTION

Here are seven tips to remember before you step into the kitchen and start cooking. Follow them as best you can to keep yourself safe while cooking, and the food you make safe to enjoy!

CHECK IN WITH AN ADULT. Speak to an adult before you start a recipe.

ARE YOU READY FOR THE UNEXPECTED? If you are using the oven, stove, or anything else that could catch on fire, be sure to have a fire extinguisher nearby.

READY YOUR CAPE. If the recipe you are making has ingredients that are messy, consider wearing an apron and definitely have towels on hand.

WASH YOUR HANDS. Also, if you have long hair, it is best to pull it back.

CRACK WITH CAUTION! There are three important safety tips about eggs: Crack an egg into its own bowl so you can scoop out any shell pieces that fall in. Raw batter that uses eggs may taste yummy, but it can make you sick—so don't eat it. And always wash your hands after touching eggs.

RINSE FRUITS AND VEGGIES. Vegetables and fruit may have been sprayed to keep bugs off of them while they were growing. To get rid of any residue or germs, be sure to rinse them thoroughly before adding them to a recipe or eating them.

DON'T LEAVE ANY EVIDENCE! That includes cleaning countertops and stovetops for spills—especially if raw meat or eggs touched them— and putting ingredients away when you're done with them. This helps to keep your surface area clean and ensure that any items that should stay cold are not out of the fridge or freezer too long.

INGREDIENTS

Before you start cooking, be sure to read through the entire recipe to make sure you have all of the ingredients (and the right amounts) on hand. You may need to look in the pantry, cupboard, fridge, freezer, or on the counter. Here is where a few common ingredients are found in your kitchen.

In the Pantry

- Almonds

- Almond butter

- Avocado oil

- Baking powder

- Black pepper

- Canned beans

- Cinnamon

- Dates

- Honey

- Maple syrup

- Olive oil

- Peanut butter

- Quinoa

- Salt

- Sugar

- Sunflower seeds

- Tomato sauce

- Vinegar

- Whole-wheat flour

In the Fridge

- Arugula

- Berries

- Cauliflower

- Cheese

- Chicken

- Eggs

- Fish

- Kale

- Peas

- Spinach

- Tofu

- Turkey

- Yogurt

In the Freezer

- Frozen fruits

- Frozen vegetables

On the Counter

- Apples

- Bananas

- Bell peppers

- Mango

- Melons

- Peaches

- Pineapple

- Plums

- Tomatoes

Grocery Store Crusade

I spy with my little eye something that is. . . Have you ever played this game with friends? It's a fun one you can play next time you're at the supermarket with your parents, grandparents, siblings, or friends.

YOU: "I spy with my little eye something that is red."

ADULT: "Is it. . . tomatoes? strawberries? apples? raspberries?"

There are so many possibilities. Try playing where you get BAM! bonus points for spying super foods. Then before you leave the store, try taking home a new fruit, vegetable, or other super food that you "spied" and haven't tried before.

KITCHEN EQUIPMENT

There are many tools in the kitchen that we can use when making a recipe. Some are small like a vegetable peeler, and some are large like an oven. Sometimes we have options between different kitchen tools. For example, when making pancakes or muffins, we can stir ingredients together by hand or we can use an electric mixer. For smoothies, we need the power of a blender. Some tools have sharp areas such as a peeler, grater, knife, and blender blade. Other tools can be very hot such as a toaster, stove, and oven. Below is a list of kitchen tools that you will see in this book. In chapter 2, we will look at how to use knives, the stove, and the oven safely. Remember that if you have questions about any of the tools, be sure to ask an adult in your home.

Tools

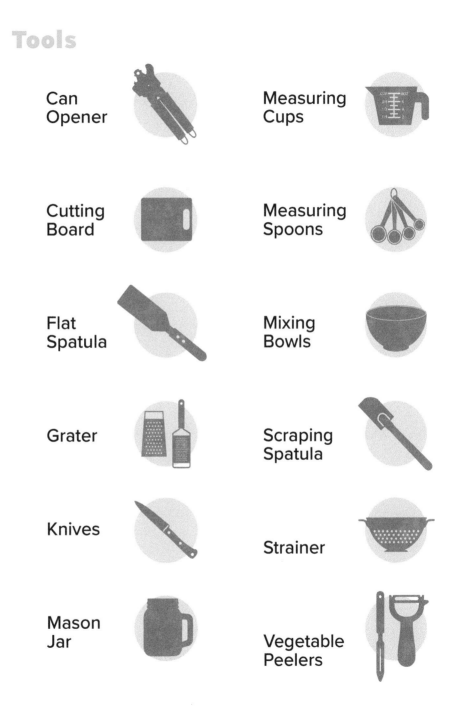

Can Opener

Measuring Cups

Cutting Board

Measuring Spoons

Flat Spatula

Mixing Bowls

Grater

Scraping Spatula

Knives

Strainer

Mason Jar

Vegetable Peelers

Whisk

Wooden or Silicone Spoon

Cookware + Bakeware

Baking Dish

Loaf Pan

Baking Sheet

Muffin Tins

Baking Stone

Pots

Frying Pan

Appliances

Blender

Oven

Hand
Mixer

Stove

Food
Processor

Toaster

COOKING SKILLS THAT SAVE THE DAY

Cooking is a wonderful way to explore new foods and nourish yourself and your family. Before starting, here are a few important lessons to get you going.

MEASURING

When you're cooking, you use ingredients such
as 2 bananas or 4 chicken breasts, but sometimes you'll need tools to
measure them. Measurements are described using numbers of cups,
ounces, tablespoons, or teaspoons. You may also see words such as
"dash" or "pinch." These are commonly used for salt, pepper, and other
strong-tasting seasonings. Both words mean "a very little bit."

When measuring ingredients, you can use measuring cups or measuring spoons. The first thing to notice is if it is a wet or dry ingredient.
This is important because there are different measuring cups for each.

Dry Measuring

Dry measuring cups typically come in the following sizes: 1 cup, ¾ cup,
⅔ cup, ½ cup, ⅓ cup, and ¼ cup. When measuring dry ingredients,
scoop the item and then use the flat side of a knife to scrape off any
extra from the top of the measuring cup.

Liquid Measuring

Liquid measuring cups come in various sizes and may hold up to 8 cups.
They are typically glass but can be plastic and they usually have a
handle on one side and a spout on the other side for easy pouring of
the liquid ingredients. When measuring, it's important to look to see that
the liquid is lining up with the correct number on the side of the liquid
measuring cup.

Measuring spoons are typically found in the following sizes: 1 tablespoon, ½ tablespoon, 1 teaspoon, ½ teaspoon, ¼ teaspoon, and
⅛ teaspoon. Measuring spoons can be used for wet or dry ingredients.

SUPER TIP

In baking, precise measurements can greatly affect the outcome of a recipe. But when cooking meals like chili or a soup, you can add more or less of the ingredients called for based on preferences. It is always best to start with small variations for any ingredient that has a strong flavor, like herbs, spices, and seasonings.

READING A RECIPE
(X-Ray Vision Not Required)

It is really important to read through a recipe from beginning to end before you start it. If you don't have all the ingredients or if you don't have time to complete all the steps, you can find another recipe.

Every recipe has a list of ingredients you will need. The order that ingredients are listed will be the order that you'll cook with them. Below the ingredients list, there are steps you will take to complete the recipe. The steps will always be listed in the order you will complete them.

Once you know that you have all the ingredients the recipe calls for, set them out on the counter along with any kitchen equipment you will need. Preparing everything before you start leads to a smooth cooking or baking experience.

Recipe Lingo

Chefs and bakers have their own words they use in recipes. Here are a few common ones you'll see and their meanings.

BAKE: Time to put it in the oven! Look at the recipe to know the oven temperature and how long to cook the food. Food is most commonly baked in a glass or ceramic dish, baking stone, baking pan, or roasting pan.

BLEND: Stir it or blend it so that the ingredients you started with magically disappear! You can "blend" with a wooden spoon, blender, or food processor.

BROIL: A lightning-fast high heat source that comes from the top. Broilers may be located inside the main oven or in a broil drawer. Please use caution when broiling. Food can burn easily.

CHOP: Cut the ingredient into pieces you could eat in one bite.

DICE: Cut the ingredient into small pieces—maybe small enough to secretly hide in a meatloaf or muffin!

MEASURE: This tells you how much of each ingredient you need; see Measuring (page 17) for more details.

MIX: Stir it or toss it!

PEEL: Take the outside layer off (like a potato's skin); usually done with a vegetable peeler or paring knife.

ROAST: Baking in a roasting pan; see "bake" above for more details.

SAUTÉ: This is a way to cook food in a frying pan on the stove—listen for the sizzle!

SCOOP: Take an amount from one container and put it into another.

SLICE: Cut into thin pieces.

SKILL 1 RECIPE
PEACHES AND CREAM SMOOTHIE

GLUTEN-FREE   NUT-FREE   VEGETARIAN

PREP TIME
5 minutes

MAKES
4
SERVINGS

TOOLS TO GATHER
blender, measuring cups

If you love peach pie and ice cream, you are going to love this smoothie! If using fresh peaches and cauliflower (as opposed to frozen), you'll want to drop 2 or 3 ice cubes into the blender. Either way, it will be creamy, delicious, and packed with nutrition.

1. **Blend ingredients.** Combine the milk, peaches, yogurt, cauliflower, dates, and ice in blender and blend on high for 2 minutes, or until smooth.

2. **Serve.** Pour into cups and enjoy.

INGREDIENTS TO HAVE:

3 cups **milk**

1 cup frozen **peaches**

1 cup **vanilla** or **peach Greek yogurt**

½ cup frozen **cauliflower**

3 pitted **dates**

THE GOOD STUFF

Adding veggies to your smoothie is a super sneaky way of getting even more veggies into your growing body. Way to go superhero!

KNIFE SKILLS

Knives are very useful in preparing ingredients to be the shape and size we desire, but they can be dangerous. **Before using a knife ask permission from an adult in your home.**

There are two ends to a knife: the handle and the blade. Then there are two sides to the blade—one is flat, and one is more rounded. The rounded side is the sharp side, and sometimes the rounded edge will have something called "a serrated edge." This gives the knife extra sharpness to cut through things like bread crust, thick peels, and raw or cooked meat.

How to Hold a Knife

When holding a knife, it is important to hold it with the blade down, so you do not harm yourself or anyone else. When starting to cut, ensure that the flat side is up, and the sharp side is facing the food. When you prepare to cut, ensure that the food is completely dry and not slippery. Then set it on a cutting board and place your thumb, pointer finger, and middle finger of your free hand firmly enough on the food that it will not slip out of your fingers, but far enough away from where the knife will cut to not cut your fingers. You might even want to use kitchen gloves. They'll keep you extra safe—and looking like you're ready to spring into action too.

SUPER TIP

Different foods require different knives based on the food's size and texture. A table knife is great for cutting most cooked food, but when preparing recipes, we often need sharper knives.

How to Slice an Apple

1. Wash and dry the apple thoroughly.

2. Choose a small- or medium-size knife with a smooth, sharp edge. These are often called "paring knives."

3. Place the apple on a cutting board with the stem facing up.

4. Hold the knife, sharp side down, with the same hand you use to write. Place your thumb and first two fingers of your free hand on the sides of the apple to hold it in place.

5. Place the point of the knife blade into the top of the apple and then press down slowly to cut the apple in half.

6. Take one half and place it with the flesh (inside) down and peel side up. Hold the apple with your free hand and use the knife to cut the apple half in half again. Repeat with the other half so that you have four pieces.

7. Place each piece with the flesh side down and cut away the core on each.

8. With the flesh side down, cut the apple quarters into as many slices as you like.

How to Chop a Tomato

1. Wash and dry the tomato thoroughly.

2. Choose a knife with a serrated edge, as tomato skin can be harder to cut through.

3. Place the tomato on a cutting board with the stem facing up.

4. Hold the knife, sharp side down, with the same hand you use to write. Place your thumb and first two fingers of your free hand on each side of the tomato to hold it in place.

5. Place the knife on the top center of the tomato and move it back and forth in ½- to 1-inch movements to cut it in half. **A**

6. Take one half and place it with the flesh (inside) down and peel side up.

7. Use your free hand to hold the tomato half in place and cut the half into slices as thick as you want the tomato to be chopped. **B**

8. Flip the tomato slices into stacks and cut the stacks into strips as wide as you want the tomato chopped.

9. Finally cut the strips across to complete the chop. **C**

A   B   C

How to Dice an Onion

1. Hold the knife, sharp side down, with the same hand you use to write. Place your thumb and first two fingers of your free hand on each side of the onion to hold it in place on its side.

2. Cut the onion in half lengthwise through the root.

3. Place the halves, cut side down, on the cutting board. Cut both ends of the onion off and peel the skin off.

4. Use your free hand to hold the onion in place and cut the halves into slices as thick as you want.

5. Flip the slices into stacks and cut crosswise. You will then have small, square pieces.

6. When you get close to your hand that is holding the onion, remove your hand and chop the remaining pieces carefully.

SKILL 2 RECIPE
RAINBOW SALAD

DAIRY-FREE   GLUTEN-FREE   NUT-FREE   VEGETARIAN

PREP TIME
5 minutes

MAKES
4
SERVINGS

TOOLS TO GATHER

cutting board, knife, mixing bowl, measuring cups

INGREDIENTS TO HAVE:

2 cups **seedless grapes**

4 **clementine oranges**

15 **strawberries**

1 **apple**

1 cup **blueberries**

THE GOOD STUFF

Your body craves the powerful goodness found in brightly colored fruits. Making a salad full of color and flavor is a fun and tasty way to give your body what it wants and needs!

This salad is so pretty. You can make it for yourself or serve it as a special treat for family and friends. And if you are looking for a pot of gold at the end of your rainbow, try serving it with a dip of plain yogurt mixed with honey or maple syrup.

1. **Wash all fruit.** Rinse the fruit well. Dry the apple and oranges with a clean cloth. Lay grapes and blueberries on a clean cloth to dry.

2. **Prepare grapes.** Cut grapes in half and place them into the bowl.

3. **Prepare oranges.** Peel the clementine oranges, pull the sections apart, and place them in the bowl.

4. **Prepare strawberries.** On a cutting board, using a small paring knife, carefully cut the stems off the top of the strawberries. Then cut each strawberry in half and place into the bowl.

5. **Prepare apple.** Dice the apple and place all the pieces in the bowl.

6. **Add blueberries.** Gently mix all ingredients together.

USING THE STOVE

If you love grilled cheese, scrambled eggs, pancakes, and pasta, then you definitely want to learn how to use a stove properly! Did you know that there are three different types of stoves? They are named for their source/delivery of heat: gas, electric, and induction.

No matter which type of stove you have, there will be knobs that you can use to turn the burners on and off. Typically, each one will offer low, medium, and high or the numbers 1 through 10. The number 1 refers to a very low temperature setting, and the number 10 refers to very hot.

When you decide to use a stovetop, you have to choose which burner you will cook on and then look for the diagram on the stove to show you which knob connects with that burner.

Remember to ask the adults in your home about the features of your stove before you use it.

Here are a few safety tips to keep in mind anytime you use a stove:

1. Let an adult know when you plan to use the stove and ensure you have their permission.

2. Use potholders when you are cooking on the stove to prevent burning your hands.

3. Oil and boiling water/sauces can splatter easily. Try using a mesh cover over the pot/pan to protect yourself from a burn and a mess.

4. Never touch a burner that has been on recently and may still be hot.

5. Stay near the stove to watch for any sign of smoke, fire, or a pot boiling over.

6. Never leave only oil in a hot pan on the stove, as it can catch fire.

7. Be sure to have a fire extinguisher accessible and in the kitchen at all times.

SUPER TIP

When it's time to use the stove remember that:

1. High heat is your best choice for boiling when you are making things like pasta.
2. Medium heat is generally your best choice for cooking things like pancakes or scrambled eggs.
3. Low is your best choice for keeping a recipe warm, like when your pasta is cooked and mixed with a sauce, but you aren't quite ready to eat supper.

✓ **MEASURING**
✓ **STOVE**

OUT-OF-THIS-WORLD OATMEAL PANCAKES

NUT-FREE   VEGETARIAN

PREP TIME
5 minutes

COOK TIME
15 to 25 minutes

MAKES
4
SERVINGS

TOOLS TO GATHER

flat spatula, frying pan, measuring cups, measuring spoons, mixing bowl

INGREDIENTS TO HAVE:

1 ripe **banana**

1 cup **milk**

⅓ cup unsweetened **applesauce**

1 **egg**

2 tablespoons **maple syrup**

1 teaspoon **vanilla extract**

1 cup **whole-wheat flour**

1 cup **rolled oats**

1 teaspoon **baking powder**

1 teaspoon **cinnamon**

These pancakes are perfect for when you need a filling breakfast, but also taste great on a night you want to make "breakfast for dinner!"

1. **Mash the banana.** Peel the banana and place it into the mixing bowl. Use a fork to mash it down.

2. **Mix the wet ingredients.** Add milk, applesauce, egg, maple syrup, and vanilla to the bowl with the mashed banana. Stir until all ingredients are mixed together.

3. **Add the dry ingredients.** Add flour, oats, baking powder, and cinnamon. Stir until all of the dry ingredients are mixed in. Set aside.

4. **Heat the pan.** 🖐 Get a nonstick frying pan and set it on one of the front burners. Carefully turn on the burner to medium heat. (If you are using a gas stove remember to ensure that the flame is lit and not just leaking gas.)

5. **Cook the pancakes.** 🖐 Pour ⅓ cup pancake mix into the pan and let it cook for 4 minutes. Once that side is cooked, carefully use a flat spatula to lift it about an inch above the pan and quickly turn it over. (A little might splatter until you get used to the "flipping motion" and that's okay!) Cook the second side for an additional 3 to 5 minutes and then use the spatula to move it to a plate.

30 *Super Foods for Super Kids Cookbook*

THE GOOD STUFF

Adding oats to pancakes helps us feel fuller longer. They have a really cool way of releasing energy slowly. This gives you super energy to get through your morning.

6. **Repeat with remaining batter.** If you have a large pan you can cook more than one or two pancakes at once, otherwise, work in batches until the batter is gone. Once complete, turn the stove off and serve.

USING THE OVEN

Now that you know how to use the stove, let's talk about ovens. If you see the words bake, roast, or broil, then you will be using an oven. Baking and roasting are more common to use. Broiling is extremely hot and fast (1 to 3 minutes) and is best used only when adults are present because foods under the broiler can burn easily.

Ovens can cook food with heat from the bottom to the top or through convection, where hot air circulates throughout. Some ovens offer both options. If this is true of your oven, it would be interesting to ask the adult in your home which they prefer to use.

SUPER TIP

Remember to ask the adults in your home about your oven before you use it. Every oven is a bit different in how it is set to heat, so this is a very important question. Here are a few tips to keep in mind anytime you use an oven:

1. Let an adult know when you plan to use the oven and ensure you have their permission.
2. Turn the oven on to the desired temperature to preheat it at least 10 minutes before anything needs to be baked.
3. Use caution by turning your face away when opening the oven, as it can let very warm air out when you first open it.
4. Use oven mitts that cover your hands and lower arms when you're placing a baking dish into the oven or removing one. And remember to never touch the inside of the oven with bare hands.
5. Stay near the oven to watch for any sign of smoke, fire, or something burning.
6. Be sure to have a fire extinguisher accessible and in the kitchen at all times.

PEANUT BUTTER PUMPKIN LOAF

✓ **MEASURING**
✓ **OVEN**

DAIRY-FREE **VEGETARIAN**

PREP TIME
10 minutes

COOK TIME
45 minutes

MAKES
10
SERVINGS

TOOLS TO GATHER

loaf pan, measuring cups, measuring spoons, mixing bowls, scraping spatula

INGREDIENTS TO HAVE:

2 **eggs**

¾ cup **peanut butter**

½ cup **pureéd pumpkin**

⅓ cup **maple syrup**

¼ cup **unsweetened applesauce**

3 tablespoons **canola oil**

½ cup **whole-wheat flour**

2 teaspoons **cinnamon**

1 teaspoon **baking powder**

½ teaspoon **nutmeg**

Peanut butter and jam, move aside; pumpkin has arrived in town! This super-moist loaf is amazing for breakfast or a quick snack. And it just might replace your PB and J sandwich from now on.

1. **Preheat oven.** Set the oven to 350° F.

2. **Mix wet ingredients.** Crack the eggs, one at a time, into a small bowl and then pour them into a mixing bowl. Add peanut butter, pumpkin, maple syrup, applesauce, and canola oil and mix until smooth and creamy.

3. **Add dry ingredients.** Add flour, cinnamon, baking powder, and nutmeg. Blend again until smooth.

4. **Transfer to loaf pan.** Pour or spoon the batter into a lightly greased loaf pan.

TO BE CONTINUED . . .

SWAP IT

Looking for a peanut-free version of this recipe? Try almond butter or pumpkin seed butter instead. Or what about a gluten-free version? Replace the whole-wheat flour with almond or coconut flour.

5. **Bake for 40 to 45 minutes.** You can test if it is done by inserting a toothpick in the center of the loaf. It will come out clean when it is finished.

6. **Remove from the oven.** Let it cool in the pan for at least 15 minutes. Run a knife along the edges to separate the loaf from the pan, then remove it from the pan and let cool entirely before slicing.

THE GOOD STUFF

Pumpkins pack a powerful punch of beta carotene. Beta carotene keeps our cells healthy and working well.

PART TWO

SUPER RECIPES

Now it is time to make recipes that are full of flavor and nutrition. If you come across an ingredient that you are not familiar with, try asking an adult about it. Cooking is a great way to learn about new foods. And if you decide that you aren't ready to try eating a new ingredient, adding it to a recipe for another member of your family is a great place to start!

MIGHTY MORNING
MUFFINS

PAGE 43

BREAKFAST

Caped Crusader Overnight Oats

Tropical Green Smoothie

Mighty Morning Muffins

Wake-Up Breakfast Cups

Let's Roll! Banana Sushi

Amazing Avocado Toast

Best Breakfast Pizza

Blueberry Blast Breakfast Cake

Marvelous Mini Egg Cups

Radical Raspberry Chia Pudding

✓ MEASURING

CAPED CRUSADER OVERNIGHT OATS

DAIRY-FREE GLUTEN-FREE VEGETARIAN

PREP TIME
10 minutes
plus
overnight
rest

MAKES
4
SERVINGS

TOOLS TO GATHER

cutting board, grater, mason jars, measuring cups, mixing bowl

INGREDIENTS TO HAVE:

1 cup **oats**

1 cup **coconut milk**

2 tablespoons **honey**

1 teaspoon **ground cinnamon**

1 **apple**

1 **carrot**

¼ cup crushed **walnuts** (optional)

Overnight oats offer a super easy breakfast because all the work is done the night before. This recipe is packed with fiber to help keep you full, beta carotene to support your eye and cell health, and omega-3 fatty acids for your growing brain.

1. **Mix dry ingredients and milk.** In a mixing bowl, combine the oats, coconut milk, honey, and ground cinnamon. Set aside.

2. **Grate apple and carrots.** Add these into the mixture and stir everything together.

3. **Pour into mason jars or other containers.** Add walnuts (if using) and place in fridge for up to 24 hours. Enjoy cold or warmed up.

THE GOOD STUFF

Did you know that when light hits your eye there is a piece that breaks off on the inside of your eye? Don't worry: Your body then replaces that piece with vitamin A. There are many foods we can get a form of vitamin A (called beta carotene) from, including carrots, pumpkin, and sweet potato. So if you've heard that carrots help you see better, it is 100 percent true!

TROPICAL GREEN SMOOTHIE

DAIRY-FREE   GLUTEN-FREE   NUT-FREE   VEGETARIAN

PREP TIME
5 minutes

MAKES

4

SERVINGS

TOOLS TO GATHER

blender, measuring cups

INGREDIENTS TO HAVE:

2 cups **coconut milk**

1 cup frozen **pineapple**

1 cup frozen **kale**

½ cup **coconut milk yogurt**

3 pitted **dates**

This vegan smoothie tastes like a tropical treat while offering lots of vitamins and minerals your body needs. The fun green color will have you feeling incredibly strong! But don't worry, you won't turn green from it.

Blend ingredients. Combine the coconut milk, pineapple, kale, yogurt, and dates in a blender and blend on high for 2 minutes, or until smooth. Pour into cups and enjoy.

THE GOOD STUFF

Dates are an amazing fruit! They are super sweet, but don't cause our blood sugar to spike like sugar does. And they contain WAY more nutrition than sugar. One really cool nutrient they offer is choline. This B vitamin has been shown to help with better memory and learning. So, gulp down this smoothie in the morning whenever you need the extra brain power at school.

MIGHTY MORNING MUFFINS

✓ MEASURING
✓ OVEN

NUT-FREE VEGETARIAN

PREP TIME
10 minutes

COOK TIME
20 to 22 minutes

MAKES
12
SERVINGS

TOOLS TO GATHER

blender, measuring cups, measuring spoons, mixing bowl, muffin tin, scraping spatula

INGREDIENTS TO HAVE:

2 large handfuls **baby spinach**

2 ripe **bananas,** peeled

6 to 8 pitted **dates**

¾ cup **vanilla Greek yogurt**

¼ cup **canola oil**

2 **eggs**

2 cups **whole-wheat flour**

1 tablespoon **baking powder**

You may not feel like a spinach salad for breakfast, but you will definitely love these spinach-packed muffins. They have a cool color, incredible taste, and are packed with all the nutrients every superhero wants to start their day.

1. **Preheat oven.** Set the oven to 375° F.

2. **Blend.** Combine the spinach, bananas, dates, yogurt, canola oil, and eggs in a food processor or blender and blend on low for 1 minute and then medium until all are blended together. Pour into a mixing bowl.

3. **Add dry ingredients.** Add the flour and baking powder and mix until you cannot see the white of the flour anymore.

4. **Scoop the batter into muffin tin.** Grease the cups of a 12-muffin tin and place about ⅓-cup portions of the batter into the cups.

TO BE CONTINUED . . .

SWAP IT

If you can't find pitted dates, try using ⅓ cup of raisins in their place.

5. **Bake muffins.** Bake for 20 to 22 minutes, or until a toothpick inserted into the middle of a muffin comes out clean. Let cool and enjoy.

THE GOOD STUFF

The spinach in these muffins adds more than a really cool color! It adds a nutrient called "iron." Iron helps your blood carry oxygen to all areas of your body and helps your brain grow strong. Other sources of iron are chicken, eggs, and black beans.

WAKE-UP BREAKFAST CUPS

DAIRY-FREE   GLUTEN-FREE   VEGETARIAN

PREP TIME
10 minutes

COOK TIME
20 to 22 minutes

MAKES

6

SERVINGS

TOOLS TO GATHER

fork, measuring cups, measuring spoons, mixing bowl, muffin tin, wooden spoon

INGREDIENTS TO HAVE:

1 ripe **banana**

1 cup **oats**

1 cup shredded **unsweetened coconut**

½ cup sliced **almonds**

¼ cup **almond butter**

¼ cup **honey**

1 teaspoon **cinnamon**

These breakfast cups are a lot like granola bars in a muffin shape. They are packed with yummy sources of fiber and protein to help keep you full until morning snack time.

1. **Preheat oven.** Set the oven to 375°F.

2. **Mash the banana.** Peel the banana and place it in a mixing bowl. Using a large fork, mash the banana.

3. **Mix in other ingredients.** Add the oats, coconut, almonds, almond butter, honey, and cinnamon and mix everything together.

4. **Scoop batter into muffin tin.** Grease the cups of a 12-cup muffin tin and place about ⅓-cup portions of batter into the cups.

5. **Bake muffins.** 🖐 Bake for 20 to 22 minutes, or until a toothpick inserted into the middle comes out clean.

THE GOOD STUFF

Oats are a great source of soluble fiber. This fiber is really cool because it helps keep us full and it acts like a vacuum to clean up things in our body to keep our hearts healthy. (Don't worry: It's not the type of vacuum that sucks everything up like when you leave a sock lying around on the floor.)

✓ KNIVES
✓ MEASURING

LET'S ROLL! BANANA SUSHI

DAIRY-FREE   VEGETARIAN

PREP TIME
5 minutes

MAKES
4
SERVING

TOOLS TO GATHER

cutting board, knife, measuring spoons

INGREDIENTS TO HAVE:

4 **whole-wheat tortillas**

8 tablespoons **nut or seed butter**

4 **bananas**, peeled

4 tablespoons **hemp hearts or flax or sesame seeds**

This breakfast sushi is super-fun to make and eat! It's perfect for a quick and easy breakfast and is packed with fiber, protein, and omega-3 fatty acids that your body craves.

1. **Spread nut or seed butter onto tortillas.** Lay the tortillas flat on a cutting board and spread 2 tablespoons of nut butter onto each one, leaving 1 to 2 inches of space from the edge.

2. **Place bananas.** Put the bananas in the center of each tortilla.

3. **Roll the tortillas up around the bananas.** Start by folding one edge in at the end of the banana, and then the other end, and then roll it closed.

4. **Slice the sushi rolls.** Using a sharp knife, cut the roll into ½-inch pieces to resemble sushi.

5. **Add the toppings.** Sprinkle with hemp hearts.

THE GOOD STUFF

Have you heard of hemp hearts? They are a really cool seed that contains a fat that helps your brain and eyes grow and develop. They also offer a great source of protein. Protein at breakfast will help you stay full longer and help your muscles grow.

AMAZING AVOCADO TOAST

NUT-FREE   VEGETARIAN

✓ KNIVES
✓ MEASURING

PREP TIME
10 minutes

COOK TIME
2 to 3 minutes

MAKES

4

SERVINGS

TOOLS TO GATHER

fork, knife, measuring spoon, mixing bowl, toaster

INGREDIENTS TO HAVE:

4 **whole-grain bread slices**

2 **avocados**

2 medium **tomatoes**

2 to 3 tablespoons grated or shredded **Parmesan cheese** (optional)

FOR LAUGHS

What did one half of the avocado say to the other half? Without you I'm empty!

This breakfast option is quick to make and very filling! It is packed with energy, fiber, and healthy fats to keep you going for hours.

1. **Make toast.** Toast the bread in the toaster.

2. **Peel and mash avocados.** 🖐 Cut each avocado in half, then remove the skin and pits. In a bowl, mash the green portion with a fork.

3. **Top the toast.** Divide the mashed avocado between the slices of toast and spread each portion onto a piece of toast.

4. **Prepare tomatoes.** 🖐 Slice into thin pieces. Place on top of the toast.

5. **Sprinkle with cheese.** Sprinkle Parmesan cheese (if using) on top and enjoy!

THE GOOD STUFF

Did you know that avocados are a fruit? They are a little different than most fruits though, because they are low in fructose (the sugar found in most fruit) and high in something called "omega-3 fatty acids," which are essential fatty acids. This means that your body cannot make these fats . . . they have to come from food. Your body is amazing at a lot of things and does a lot for you, so here is a great way that you do something for it and give it a nutrient it cannot make. Yay!

BEST BREAKFAST PIZZA

✓ KNIVES
✓ MEASURING
✓ STOVE

NUT-FREE   VEGETARIAN

PREP TIME
5 minutes

COOK TIME
15 minutes

MAKES
4
SERVINGS

TOOLS TO GATHER

cutting board, flat spatula, frying pan, grater, knife, measuring cup, mixing bowl, toaster

INGREDIENTS TO HAVE:

8 **eggs**

4 **English muffins**

4 ounces **cheese**

2 **avocados**

1 cup **tomato sauce** or **ketchup**

Pizza for breakfast? Yes, please! These personal pizzas offer a great source of fiber, protein, calcium, and iron to start your day off with a bang.

1. **Cook eggs.** Place a nonstick frying pan on one of the front burners on your stove and turn it to medium heat. Carefully crack eggs, one at a time, into a small bowl, and pour them into the pan as you go. After doing this with all 8 eggs, proceed to step 2 starting with the first egg you cracked.

2. **Flip eggs.** After 4 to 5 minutes, you will notice that the outer portion of the egg turns from clear to white. That is your cue that it is time to turn the eggs over one at a time. Using a flat spatula, cut through the egg whites to make space to start flipping the eggs. Carefully slip the spatula under each one and, when you are ready, quickly flip them over. If some of the yolk spills out, no worries. It all tastes the same.

3. **Toast English muffins.** While the eggs finish cooking, toast the English muffins.

TO BE CONTINUED . . .

THE GOOD STUFF

Did you know that nutrients sometimes work together? Take Vitamin C: It helps your body absorb iron. This means that the vitamin C in the tomato sauce of this recipe helps your body absorb iron from the avocado and eggs. Yay for team players!

4. **Prepare cheese and avocado.** Grate the cheese. Cut avocado in half, remove the skin and pit, and dice the green flesh.

5. **Create pizzas.** Once everything is ready, add the tomato sauce to the English muffins, then sprinkle with grated cheese, add an egg to each, and top with avocado.

BLUEBERRY BLAST BREAKFAST CAKE

NUT-FREE   VEGETARIAN

PREP TIME
10 to 15 minutes

COOK TIME
35 to 40 minutes

MAKES
12
SERVINGS

TOOLS TO GATHER

baking dish, fork, measuring cups, measuring spoons, mixing bowls, wooden spoon

INGREDIENTS TO HAVE:

2 cups **whole-wheat flour**

1 teaspoon **ground cinnamon**

1 teaspoon **baking powder**

2 **eggs**

1 cup **milk**

⅓ cup **unsweetened applesauce**

⅓ cup **canola oil**

¼ cup **maple syrup**

2 cups frozen **blueberries**

When food tastes this good, you wonder how you ever lived without it. This cake is so yummy and packed with vitamin C and other antioxidants to help you fight off any germs that might be around.

1. **Preheat oven.** Set the oven to 350° F.

2. **Mix dry ingredients.** Measure the flour, ground cinnamon, and baking powder into a bowl and stir together.

3. **Mix wet ingredients.** Crack the eggs, one at a time, into a small bowl. Check for any pieces of shell (remove any you find) and then transfer the eggs to a large bowl. Add the milk, applesauce, oil, and maple syrup. Mix wet ingredients until they are blended.

4. **Mix all ingredients together.** Add the flour mixture to wet mixture. Once a batter is formed, add blueberries and stir a few times. Try to not overmix and smash the berries.

TO BE CONTINUED . . .

FLAVOR BOOST

Do you like icing on your cake? Add a little Greek yogurt or your favorite nut or seed butter when you serve this up.

5. **Bake the cake.** Pour the mixture into a greased 8-by-8-inch baking dish. Place in the oven for 35 to 40 minutes, or until a toothpick inserted in the center comes out clean.

THE GOOD STUFF

Blueberries are packed with antioxidants. That is a big word that basically means "sickness fighters." Blueberries, along with other dark-colored fruit, help keep away colds and flus and if we do get sick, they help us get better faster. You can add blueberries to baked goods like this cake, or add them to your oatmeal or favorite smoothie.

MARVELOUS MINI EGG CUPS

GLUTEN-FREE   NUT-FREE   VEGETARIAN

PREP TIME
15 minutes

COOK TIME
20 minutes

MAKES
6
SERVINGS

TOOLS TO GATHER

knife, measuring cups, measuring spoons, mini-muffin tin, mixing bowls, whisk

INGREDIENTS TO HAVE:

6 **eggs**

1 **bell pepper**

3 ounces **cheese**

½ cup **milk**

1 tablespoon **honey mustard**

These bite-size treats are packed with protein, iron, and vitamin C to support amazing growth and development. Oh, and they taste great too!

1. **Preheat oven.** Set the oven to 400°F.

2. **Whisk eggs.** Crack the eggs, one at a time, into a small bowl. Check for any pieces of shell (remove any you find) and then transfer the eggs to a large bowl. Whisk for 1 to 2 minutes, until they are a bit fluffy.

3. **Prep bell pepper and cheese.** Cut the bell pepper in half and remove the seeds and core. Dice the pepper and grate the cheese.

4. **Mix ingredients together.** Add the pepper, cheese, milk, and honey mustard to the eggs. Mix together gently.

5. **Fill muffin tin.** Grease the cups of a 12-cup muffin tin and pour mixture into the cups. Then check to ensure that there is even distribution of cheese and peppers throughout the sections.

TO BE CONTINUED . . .

6. **Bake.** Place in the oven for 20 minutes, until the eggs are set. Let cool for 5 minutes before removing from the pan.

THE GOOD STUFF

Eggs, milk, and cheese are all great sources of protein. Your body uses protein to grow and repair muscles. Other sources of protein are fish, chickpeas, and black beans.

RADICAL RASPBERRY CHIA PUDDING

✓ MEASURING

DAIRY-FREE   GLUTEN-FREE   NUT-FREE   VEGETARIAN

PREP TIME
5 minutes, plus 6 to 8 hours to soak

MAKES
4
SERVINGS

TOOLS TO GATHER
blender, mason jars, measuring cups, measuring spoons

This recipe is a bit like a science experiment. You have to be patient while you wait for the chia seeds to grow in size as they soak up moisture from the milk. Once it is done, it is a great breakfast to enjoy at home or on the go.

1. **Blend ingredients.** Blend the coconut milk and raspberries in a blender. Set aside.

2. **Fill jars.** Add 2 tablespoons each of chia seeds and coconut to the bottom of 4 mason jars. Pour the raspberry coconut milk over all the other ingredients and stir.

3. **Let it soak.** Place into the fridge for 6 to 8 hours and enjoy.

INGREDIENTS TO HAVE:

4 cups **coconut milk**

2 cups fresh or frozen **raspberries**

8 tablespoons **chia seeds**

8 tablespoons **shredded coconut**

SWAP IT
You can make this recipe with any fresh or frozen fruit you love. Try mango, banana, blueberries, or combine some of your favorite fruits together.

THE GOOD STUFF

Chia seeds are an incredible package of protein. Did you know that protein is a bit like a LEGO? Amino acids in food are a certain shape. Then when you digest them, your body pulls that shape apart, and puts the amino acids back together as a body protein. Thank goodness our bodies have directions for that.

AWESOME
APPLE NACHOS

PAGE **58**

SNACKS

✓ KNIVES
✓ MEASURING

AWESOME APPLE NACHOS

GLUTEN-FREE   VEGETARIAN

PREP TIME
5 minutes

MAKES
4
SERVINGS

TOOLS TO GATHER

cutting board, knife, measuring spoons

INGREDIENTS TO HAVE:

¾ cup **plain** or **vanilla yogurt**

¼ cup **honey** or **maple syrup**

4 **apples**

½ cup sliced **almonds**

1 tablespoon **cinnamon**

FLAVOR BOOST

Try adding granola for added crunch and flavor.

Apples make a great snack because they are sweet, crunchy, and packed with nutrition. But sometimes you want something more than just an apple on the go. For those times, these apple nachos are perfect! They are pretty to look at and have added protein from the yogurt and almonds.

1. **Make the sauce.** Mix yogurt and honey together and set aside.

2. **Slice apples.** Slice apples into several pieces and arrange on a platter in a thin layer.

3. **Make nachos.** Drizzle yogurt mixture over top, then top with almonds and cinnamon.

THE GOOD STUFF

"An apple a day keeps the doctor away!" Have you heard this saying and wondered if it is true? Well, to an extent it is! Apples are full of fiber, which keeps your heart and intestines healthy, and antioxidants to help you get sick less often.

ON-THE-GO TRAIL MIX

✓ MEASURING

DAIRY-FREE   VEGETARIAN

PREP TIME
5 to 10 minutes

MAKES
10
SERVINGS

TOOLS TO GATHER
measuring cups, mixing bowl, wooden or silicone spoon

INGREDIENTS TO HAVE:

1 cup **Chex cereal**

1 cup **Multi Grain Cheerios**

½ cup **almonds**

½ cup **raisins**

½ cup **dried cranberries**

½ cup **pumpkin seeds**

½ cup **sunflower seeds**

½ cup **dark chocolate chips**

SWAP IT Try using additional or alternate cereals, dried fruit, or seeds to make up your own version of trail mix.

This is a great snack mix to enjoy between school and sports practice. You can store it in a large container or in several small ones for an easy grab-and-go option.

1. **Measure out all ingredients.** Using a ½ cup measuring cup, scoop all ingredients into a large bowl or container.

2. **Mix with a large spoon.** Enjoy in ½ cup portions.

THE GOOD STUFF

Grains and nuts/seeds are like puzzle pieces that fit together perfectly. Each one is missing nutrients that the other one has. Enjoy them together to complete the puzzle.

ZIPPY ZUCCHINI CHOCOLATE CHIP COOKIES

DAIRY-FREE GLUTEN-FREE NUT-FREE VEGETARIAN

PREP TIME
15 minutes

COOK TIME
12 to 14 minutes

MAKES
10
SERVINGS

TOOLS TO GATHER

baking stone/ baking sheet, cutting board, grater, measuring cups, measuring spoons, mixing bowl

INGREDIENTS TO HAVE:

1 medium **zucchini**

½ cup **pumpkin seed butter**

½ cup **honey**

1 teaspoon **vanilla extract**

2 cups **rolled oats**

¾ cup shredded **unsweetened coconut**

½ cup unsalted **pumpkin seeds**

½ cup mini **dark chocolate chips**

1 teaspoon **ground cinnamon**

1 teaspoon **baking powder**

These cookies are a twist on your grandma's chocolate chip cookie. They are just as yummy but packed with the goodness of pumpkin seeds and zucchini too!

1. **Preheat oven.** Set the oven to 375°F.

2. **Shred the zucchini.** 🖐 Wash zucchini and shred it until you have 1 cup of shredded zucchini. Pour it into a large mixing bowl.

3. **Mix in the wet ingredients.** Add in pumpkin seed butter, honey, and vanilla and mix together.

4. **Add dry ingredients.** Add all the remaining ingredients in the following order, mixing after each addition. Add oats, coconut, pumpkin seeds, chocolate chips, ground cinnamon, and baking powder.

5. **Make cookies.** Form small balls, using about 2 tablespoons each, and place on baking stone or baking sheet.

TO BE CONTINUED . . .

THE GOOD STUFF

Pumpkin seed butter and pumpkin seeds offer a fun addition of crunch and nutrition to cookies. They are especially high in magnesium which is a mineral that keeps our bones strong and helps us get a good night's sleep. Maybe that makes these cookies ideal for a late snack!

6. **Bake cookies.** Place in the oven for 12 to 14 minutes, until they are slightly brown on the edges and top.

STONE FRUIT SALAD

✓ KNIVES
✓ MEASURING

DAIRY-FREE   GLUTEN-FREE   NUT-FREE   VEGETARIAN

PREP TIME
15 to 20 minutes

MAKES
6
SERVINGS

TOOLS TO GATHER

cutting board, knives, measuring spoons, mixing bowl

INGREDIENTS TO HAVE:

3 tablespoons **maple syrup**

1 teaspoon **vanilla extract**

3 **plums**

2 **peaches**

2 **nectarines**

1 cup **grapes**

4 **mint leaves**

QUICK TIP

Cutting up fruit can be dangerous because it is slippery. Be sure to watch your knife carefully, go slow, and ask for help as needed while cutting the fruit up.

Have you heard the term "stone fruit?" This is the name given to fruit that has a fleshy portion on the outside and then a pit in the middle with a seed inside of it. Stone fruits make a wonderful and juicy snack.

1. **Make sauce.** Combine the maple syrup and vanilla in a small bowl and set aside.

2. **Prepare fruit.** Cut the plums, peaches, and nectarines open and remove the pit from each one. Chop the plums, peaches, nectarines, and grapes into bite-size pieces and place in a bowl.

3. **Mix salad together.** Drizzle the sauce over top and mix everything together.

4. **Top with mint leaves.** Cut the mint leaves into small pieces and sprinkle on top.

THE GOOD STUFF

Did you know that mint helps to reduce gas in your body and helps with bad breath too?! So, I guess you will be smelling great after enjoying this salad.

KALE CHIPS FOR CHAMPS

✓ MEASURING
✓ OVEN

DAIRY-FREE GLUTEN-FREE NUT-FREE VEGETARIAN

PREP TIME
10 minutes

COOK TIME
10 to 12 minutes

MAKES
4
SERVINGS

TOOLS TO GATHER

baking stone/ baking sheet, measuring spoons

INGREDIENTS TO HAVE:

1 large bunch **kale**

2 tablespoons **avocado oil**

2 tablespoons **nutritional yeast**

Okay, it's time to leave the bags of chips at the grocery store and make your own! Kale chips are fun, crunchy, and packed with nutrition. Enjoy them as a snack or with a sandwich or burger.

1. **Preheat oven.** Set the oven to 400°F.

2. **Wash and dry kale.** Pull kale leaves apart and rinse them well with cold water. Pat dry with a clean kitchen towel.

3. **Prepare kale for roasting.** Tear the kale into pieces about 3 to 4 inches across and place it on the baking stone or baking sheet in a single layer.

4. **Add the seasonings.** Drizzle the oil over the kale, and then sprinkle the nutritional yeast.

TO BE CONTINUED . . .

5. **Roast the kale chips.** Bake for about 10 to 12 minutes until crunchy. Watch them closely to prevent burning. Carefully remove from the oven.

THE GOOD STUFF

Kale is packed with beta carotene and vitamin K. Beta carotene can be changed into vitamin A in the body. It helps our eyes, bones, and cells stay healthy. Vitamin K helps our blood to clot if we get a cut or scrape.

QUINOA ENERGY BITES

DAIRY-FREE   GLUTEN-FREE   VEGETARIAN

PREP TIME
20 minutes

COOK TIME
5 minutes

MAKES
6
SERVINGS

TOOLS TO GATHER

baking sheet, food processor, measuring cups, measuring spoons

INGREDIENTS TO HAVE:

⅔ cup **water**

⅓ cup dry **quinoa**

1 cup **rolled oats**

½ cup **raisins**

½ cup **peanut butter**

½ cup **sunflower seeds**

⅓ cup **honey**

1 teaspoon **ground cinnamon**

These no-bake energy bites are easy to make and packed with protein, fiber, and fast-acting energy. They are a perfect lunch-box snack too!

1. **Cook quinoa.** Place the water and quinoa in a small pot. Bring to a boil over high heat. Once boiling, reduce heat to a simmer and cover. Let simmer for 12 minutes or until all water is absorbed. Remove from heat, fluff with a fork, and set aside.

2. **Mix ingredients together.** Combine the cooked quinoa, oats, raisins, peanut butter, sunflower seeds, honey, and ground cinnamon in a food processor and mix on low until the ingredients are blended well.

3. **Roll into bite-size pieces.** Form into small balls, using about 2 tablespoons each, and place on parchment paper–lined baking sheet.

4. **Refrigerate for 1 hour.** Then remove and store in an airtight container.

THE GOOD STUFF

Quinoa is a grain that is packed with protein. Protein is important every day to help your body repair muscles and other body tissue.

✓ MEASURING
✓ OVEN

CRISPY CRUNCHY CHICKPEAS

DAIRY-FREE GLUTEN-FREE NUT-FREE VEGETARIAN

PREP TIME
10 minutes

COOK TIME
1 hour

MAKES
6
SERVINGS

TOOLS TO GATHER

baking sheet, mixing bowl, strainer

INGREDIENTS TO HAVE:

1 (15-ounce) can **chickpeas**

2 tablespoons **avocado oil**

2 tablespoons **maple syrup**

1 teaspoon **cinnamon**

This crunchy snack is great on its own, but also makes a great yogurt topper or can be added to your favorite trail mix.

1. **Preheat oven.** Set the oven to 350° F.

2. **Prepare chickpeas.** Pour chickpeas from the can into a strainer. Rinse well and place onto a clean kitchen towel. Once dry, place them in a bowl and toss with avocado oil. Pour them onto a greased baking stone or baking sheet.

3. **Roast chickpeas.** Place chickpeas in the oven and roast for 45 minutes. Pull the baking stone out, and stir the chickpeas around a little bit halfway through.

4. **Remove from oven.** Place roasted chickpeas in a mixing bowl and add maple syrup and cinnamon. Toss again until evenly coated and return to the baking stone.

5. **Return to oven.** Bake for another 10 to 15 minutes. Let cool and enjoy!

THE GOOD STUFF

Chickpeas are a source of fiber and protein. Snacks high in these two nutrients help us stay fuller longer.

MELON
SUPER SLUSHY

✓ KNIVES
✓ MEASURING

GLUTEN-FREE   NUT-FREE   VEGETARIAN

PREP TIME
10 minutes

MAKES
4
SERVINGS

**TOOLS
TO GATHER**

cutting board, blender, knife, measuring cups, measuring spoon

INGREDIENTS TO HAVE:

½ **honeydew melon**

1 **cucumber**

1 cup **Greek yogurt**

1 cup **ice**

2 tablespoon **maple syrup**

This refreshing slushy is perfect for a hot summer afternoon or after any sports, gymnastics, or dance practice. It's also great paired with the Crispy Crunchy Chickpeas found on page 68.

1. **Dice melon and cucumber.** 🖐 Carefully cut melon and cucumber into 1-inch pieces until you have 2 cups of each. Discard melon rinds and seeds.

2. **Blend ingredients.** Add melon, cucumber, yogurt, ice, and maple syrup to the blender, and process for 1 minute, until smooth. Pour into cups and enjoy.

THE GOOD STUFF

Did you know that cucumbers are 96 percent water? And honeydew melon is 90 percent water! Having enough water in our body is really important as it helps us focus, digest food well, and it keeps our body temperature at the right place. If you are struggling to get enough water in each day, try adding this slushy to your snack time routine.

✓ MEASURING

ALMOND BUTTER AND DATE BOATS

DAIRY-FREE   GLUTEN-FREE   VEGETARIAN

PREP TIME
5 minutes

MAKES
4
SERVINGS

TOOLS TO GATHER

measuring spoon

INGREDIENTS TO HAVE:

12 pitted **dates**

½ cup **almond butter**

SWAP IT
If you don't have dates, try making these with figs. If you don't have almond butter, use whatever nut or seed butter you have in the house.

Sometimes you need a little snack with lots of power packed inside. These "boats" are the perfect choice. They're loaded with energy and flavor to keep you going until your next meal.

1. **Prepare dates.** Carefully open dates to ensure that dates do not have pits and lay them down slightly opened.

2. **Add almond butter.** Add 2 teaspoons almond butter into the center of each date and enjoy.

THE GOOD STUFF
Almond butter is a great source of calcium. Calcium helps our bones grow longer and stronger.

PROTEIN-PACKED BROWNIES

VEGETARIAN

PREP TIME
15 minutes

COOK TIME
20 to 25 minutes

MAKES
12
SERVINGS

TOOLS TO GATHER

baking dish, measuring cups, measuring spoon, mixing bowl, scraping spatula, wooden spoon

INGREDIENTS TO HAVE:

2 cups **vanilla Greek yogurt** (2 percent fat or higher)

2 cups **peanut butter**

2 tablespoons **maple syrup**

½ cup **cocoa powder**

1 cup shredded **unsweetened coconut**

1 cup **whole-wheat flour**

These protein-packed brownies are great for times when you want something sweet that comes with good muscle and bone-building nutrition.

1. **Preheat oven.** Set the oven to 350°F.

2. **Mix wet ingredients.** Stir yogurt, peanut butter, and maple syrup together.

3. **Add dry ingredients.** Mix in cocoa powder, then shredded coconut, then flour.

4. **Pour batter into pan.** Transfer batter to a greased 8-by-8-inch baking dish.

5. **Bake the brownies.** Bake for about 20 to 25 minutes, until a knife inserted in the center comes out clean.

THE GOOD STUFF

Cocoa is a form of chocolate, but it is less sweet than the chocolate you are likely used to. And while chocolate may get a bad reputation at times, cocoa is actually very good for you. It can keep your cells and tissues healthy and causes things to be released in your brain and help you relax. So, who says you can't stay healthy and enjoy a chocolate treat? Not me! But try to make it one that has pure cocoa and added protein and fiber too.

CHICKPEA-STUFFED
PEPPERS

PAGE **88**

LUNCH

Turbo Turkey Wrap

Ba-Bam! Bagel Pizza

Cheesy Carrot Quesadillas

Speedy Salmon Bites

Eggy Boats

Magic Tuna Melt

Creamy Tomato Soup

Sweet Potato Pancakes

Greek Salad

Trail Mix Salad

Chickpea-Stuffed Peppers

TURBO TURKEY WRAP

DAIRY-FREE   NUT-FREE

PREP TIME
5 minutes

MAKES
4
SERVINGS

TOOLS TO GATHER

measuring cups, measuring spoons, mixing bowl, small spoon

INGREDIENTS TO HAVE:

¼ cup **hummus**

2 tablespoons **honey mustard**

4 large **whole-grain wraps**

8 ounces **turkey**

2 cups **mixed greens**

SWAP IT

Looking for a vegan option? You can replace the turkey with thin slices of extra firm tofu or warmed tempeh.

Short on time? This quick and easy lunch is perfect for at home, school, or on the go. Pair it with cut-up carrots, hummus, and an apple and you are good to go.

1. **Prepare the spread.** Mix together hummus and honey mustard in a small bowl.

2. **Make the wraps.** Lay the wraps on a plate or cutting board. Add the spread to each, then divide the turkey and greens between the wraps. Roll them up and enjoy.

THE GOOD STUFF

Hummus is a really cool dip made from chickpeas, sesame seed butter (also known as tahini), lemon juice, olive oil, and garlic. It is full of fiber and flavor. In this recipe we are using it as a spread, but it is also great with cut-up carrots and cucumber for a snack.

BA-BAM! BAGEL PIZZA

✓ KNIVES
✓ MEASURING
✓ OVEN

NUT-FREE

PREP TIME
10 minutes

COOK TIME
10 minutes

MAKES
4
SERVINGS

TOOLS TO GATHER

baking stone/ baking sheet, cutting board, grater, knives, measuring cup

INGREDIENTS TO HAVE:

2 **whole-grain bagels**

12 ounces **ham**

8 ounces **mozzarella cheese**

½ cup **tomato sauce**

Move over, bagel and cream cheese . . . there are pizza toppings in town. These personal pizzas will quickly become a favorite for everyone in your home.

1. **Preheat oven.** Set the oven to 350°F.

2. **Prepare ingredients.** Cut bagels in half so that the inside is open in the shape of an "O." Dice ham and shred cheese.

3. **Make pizzas.** Spread tomato sauce on the inside of the bagels. Add ham, then cheese.

4. **Bake pizzas.** Place the bagel pizzas on a baking stone or baking sheet and cook for 10 to 12 minutes, until the cheese is melted.

5. **Remove from oven.** Let cool for 5 minutes before serving. Serve with a side of fresh veggies and dip.

THE GOOD STUFF

Is there is difference between whole wheat and whole grain? YES! There is this tiny portion of a grain called "the germ." It is packed with protein, vitamins, minerals, and healthy fats. When we choose whole grain, the germ is there. When we choose whole wheat this nutrition powerhouse has been excluded. So, it's time to get on the whole grain train!

CHEESY CARROT QUESADILLAS

NUT-FREE   VEGETARIAN

PREP TIME
10 minutes

COOK TIME
5 minutes

MAKES
4
SERVINGS

TOOLS TO GATHER

cutting board, grater, measuring cup, mixing bowl, vegetable peeler

INGREDIENTS TO HAVE:

8 ounces **cheese**

2 **carrots**

4 large **whole-wheat wraps**

FLAVOR BOOST

Skip the ketchup and try serving these with homemade guacamole. Just mash down a pitted and peeled avocado, and add a drop of olive oil and a squeeze of fresh lime juice. Delish!

There is nothing quite like freshly melted cheese in a sandwich or quesadilla. These are a lot like grilled cheese, but with more nutrition for strong bones and eyesight.

1. **Preheat oven.** Set the oven to 350°F.

2. **Prep the cheese and carrots.** Grate the cheese. Wash, peel, and grate the carrots.

3. **Make the quesadillas.** Lay the wraps flat on a plate or cutting board. Add one-quarter of the carrots and cheese to each one and then fold them in half. Place on a baking sheet and cook in the oven for 10 to 12 minutes, until the edges are golden brown in color.

4. **Serve and enjoy.** Remove the quesadillas from the oven and let cool for 5 minutes, then cut into triangles.

THE GOOD STUFF

Did you know that by the time you are 19 years old 90 percent of your bone is made? And by 30, it is all made. Calcium and protein are really important for growing strong bones. Cheese is a great source of both. So, load up those quesadillas and feel your bones grow long and strong.

SPEEDY SALMON BITES

DAIRY-FREE   NUT-FREE

PREP TIME
10 minutes

MAKES
4
SERVINGS

TOOLS TO GATHER

can opener, cutting board, knife, measuring spoon, mixing spoon

INGREDIENTS TO HAVE:

1 **celery stalk**

2 **cucumbers**

2 (5-ounce) cans **salmon**

4 tablespoons **mayonnaise**

FLAVOR BOOST

Want something even more crunchy? Spoon a little salmon salad onto your favorite crackers.

Tired of sandwiches? Then these bite-size stacks are for you! The combination of crunchy cucumber and creamy salmon salad is delicious. If you don't have salmon on hand, tuna salad or egg salad will work too.

1. **Wash and prepare vegetables.** Wash celery and dice it into small pieces. Wash cucumber and slice it in circles about a ½-inch thick.

2. **Make salmon salad.** Open the cans of salmon and drain the liquid from the cans. Put the salmon into a mixing bowl and mix it with mayonnaise and celery.

3. **Make stacks.** Scoop 1 to 2 tablespoons of salmon salad onto cucumber slices and serve.

THE GOOD STUFF

Celery is a great source of potassium. Potassium is a mineral that your body uses to keep fluids both in and out of the cells in proper amounts. This may sound simple, but it's actually not. If we have too much fluid in or out of the cells it can be a medical emergency. So, get crunching on that celery any chance you get. Other great sources of potassium are oranges and bananas.

EGGY BOATS

DAIRY-FREE   GLUTEN-FREE   NUT-FREE   VEGETARIAN

PREP TIME
10 minutes

COOK TIME
6 minutes

MAKES
4
SERVINGS

TOOLS TO GATHER

cutting board, knife, measuring spoons, mixing bowl, pot

INGREDIENTS TO HAVE:

6 **eggs**

1 **avocado**

1 tablespoon **Dijon mustard**

1 tablespoon **lemon juice**

4 snack-size **peppers**

Get ready to set sail to delicious town! These egg salad boats are a fun alternative to egg salad sandwiches. Can you think of fun creative ways to serve them, so it looks like they are on water?

1. **Boil eggs.** Place eggs in a pot of cold water, bring to a boil, then simmer for 12 minutes. Run under cold water to cool. Peel the eggs and chop roughly.

2. **Prepare sauce.** Peel and mash avocado. Mix in the Dijon mustard and lemon juice.

3. **Make egg salad.** In a bowl, mash and combine boiled eggs and sauce.

4. **Make boats.** Cut peppers in half and remove seeds. Scoop the egg salad into the cavity of the peppers and enjoy.

THE GOOD STUFF

Lemon juice is pretty cool. It has vitamin C, which is also called "ascorbic acid." This acid helps protect us from sickness and helps protect food from browning. So, by adding a dash of lemon juice to the egg salad, you AND the avocado will benefit. Talk about efficiency!

✓ KNIVES
✓ MEASURING
✓ OVEN

MAGIC TUNA MELT

NUT-FREE

PREP TIME
10 minutes

COOK TIME
5 minutes

MAKES
4
SERVINGS

TOOLS TO GATHER

baking sheet, can opener, cutting board, knife, measuring spoon, mixing bowl, mixing spoon, toaster

INGREDIENTS TO HAVE:

1 **celery** stalk

2 (5-ounce) cans **tuna**

4 tablespoons **mayonnaise**

4 **English muffins**

4 **Swiss cheese** slices

Tuna melts are a fun open-faced sandwich option for days that you have time to make lunch at home. You can make a cold version without melting the cheese if you are packing these in a lunch box.

1. **Preheat oven.** Set the oven to 350°F.

2. **Dice the celery.** 🖐 Wash and dry the celery stalk and then cut it into small pieces.

3. **Make the tuna salad.** Open the cans of tuna, drain the liquid, and place the tuna in a bowl. Add the mayonnaise and diced celery and mix together.

4. **Toast the English muffins.** Place in toaster on the light-medium setting.

SWAP IT

If you don't have tuna on hand, you can also make this recipe with leftover chicken breast, salmon, or eggs.

5. **Make the melts.** When the English muffins are toasted, place on a baking sheet. Spread the tuna on top and then place one piece of Swiss cheese over each tuna sandwich. Bake for 8 to 10 minutes, or until cheese is melted. Remove and enjoy once slightly cooled.

THE GOOD STUFF

"Everything in moderation." This is a really important phrase in all areas of food. In this recipe, it applies to the tuna. Tuna is a wonderful source of protein and iron, but it also contains mercury and other contaminants that aren't great for us in large quantities. For this reason, it is good to enjoy tuna or other fish two to three times per week. The FDA advises smaller tuna like skipjack is a better choice over larger tuna, such as albacore and bigeye.

CREAMY TOMATO SOUP

DAIRY-FREE · GLUTEN-FREE · NUT-FREE · VEGETARIAN

PREP TIME
10 minutes

COOK TIME
15 minutes

MAKES
4
SERVINGS

TOOLS TO GATHER

baking sheet, blender/food processor, measuring cups, pot, measuring spoons, knife, cutting board

INGREDIENTS TO HAVE:

7 **tomatoes**

2 **sweet onions**

4 **garlic cloves**

1 tablespoon **avocado oil**

2 cups **vegetable broth**

1 tablespoon **dried thyme**

1 teaspoon **dried oregano**

8 **basil leaves**

1 cup **coconut milk**

This soup is a perfect weekend lunch that keeps on giving all week long. Store it in the fridge or freezer and warm it up for a thermos lunch any day of the week.

1. **Preheat oven.** Set the oven to 400° F.

2. **Roast tomatoes, onions, and garlic.** 🖐 Wash and dice tomatoes. Peel and dice onions and garlic. Place on large baking sheet, then toss them in the avocado oil. Bake for 40 to 50 minutes, until softened.

3. **Prepare the broth.** 🖐 In the meantime, add the vegetable broth, thyme, oregano, and basil leaves to a large pot.

4. **Make the soup.** When the veggies are done roasting, add them to the pot and stir in the coconut milk too.

5. **Blend the soup.** Transfer mixture to blender and blend in batches until pureéd. Ensure you leave a place for the steam to escape to avoid the lid bursting off during blending.

6. **Heat the soup.** Transfer pureéd soup back to stock pot and warm through over medium-low heat.

THE GOOD STUFF

Basil is an amazing herb. It is packed with antioxidants to fight off illness, and it changes in flavor depending on whether it is fresh or dried or cooked. Also, its name comes from a word that means "royal," making this soup fit for a king and queen!

✓ KNIVES
✓ MEASURING
✓ STOVE

SWEET POTATO PANCAKES

DAIRY-FREE GLUTEN-FREE NUT-FREE VEGETARIAN

PREP TIME
10 minutes

COOK TIME
20 minutes

MAKES
4
SERVINGS

TOOLS TO GATHER

cutting board, frying pan, knife, measuring cup, measuring spoons, mixing bowl, pot, vegetable peeler, whisk

INGREDIENTS TO HAVE:

4 **sweet potatoes**

8 **eggs**

¼ cup **maple syrup**

1 teaspoon **cinnamon**

2 tablespoons **coconut oil**

These pancakes are a twist on traditional pancakes because they are packed with veggies! They are a great choice for any meal of the day.

1. **Prepare sweet potatoes.** Peel the sweet potatoes and dice into small cubes.

2. **Cook sweet potatoes.** Fill a saucepan with 2 inches of water and bring to a boil. Drop the sweet potato in, cover, and steam for 7 minutes or until tender when pierced with a fork. Drain the liquid, transfer the steamed sweet potatoes to a bowl, and mash with a fork.

3. **Make pancakes.** Crack the eggs, one at a time, into a small bowl. Check for any pieces of shell (remove any you find) and then transfer the eggs to a large bowl. Whisk eggs and mix them with the mashed sweet potato, maple syrup, and cinnamon.

4. **Cook the pancakes.** Melt coconut oil in a large skillet over medium heat. Once hot, pour pancakes in the skillet, about a ¼ cup of batter at a time. Cook each side for 3 to 5 minutes, flipping once, until browned.

THE GOOD STUFF

Sweet potatoes are a wonderful source of beta carotene that the body can convert to vitamin A. It also plays a cool part in helping our cells work properly. Can you imagine if you had a car but no key? You could never use it! That's how the body feels without enough vitamin A. It has the cells, but without vitamin A, the key isn't there for them to work properly.

GREEK SALAD

GLUTEN-FREE NUT-FREE VEGETARIAN

PREP TIME
10 minutes

MAKES
4
SERVINGS

TOOLS TO GATHER

cutting board, knife, mixing bowl, mason jar, measuring cups, measuring spoons

INGREDIENTS TO HAVE:

1 **romaine lettuce** head

1 **red onion**

1 **cucumber**

2 **tomatoes**

3 tablespoons **olive oil**

2 tablespoons **lemon juice**

2 tablespoons **honey**

1 cup crumbled **feta cheese**

½ cup pitted **black olives**

This salad is packed with antioxidants, color, and flavor. You can also make it into a pasta salad by replacing the romaine lettuce with your favorite pasta.

1. **Prepare lettuce.** Wash and dry the lettuce well. Tear it into bite-size pieces.

2. **Prepare other vegetables.** Peel and dice onion, then wash and dice cucumber and tomatoes.

3. **Make the dressing.** Mix oil, lemon juice, and honey together in a mason jar or glass container with a lid. Shake well.

4. **Make the salad.** In a large bowl, toss the lettuce, onion, cucumber, and tomatoes in the dressing. Top with feta cheese and black olives.

THE GOOD STUFF

Tomatoes contain something called "lycopene." Lycopene has been shown to protect against sun damage and several types of cancer. Lycopene can also be found in watermelon and papayas.

TRAIL MIX SALAD

GLUTEN-FREE   DAIRY-FREE   VEGETARIAN

PREP TIME
10 minutes

COOK TIME
10 minutes

MAKES
4
SERVINGS

TOOLS TO GATHER

mixing bowl, mason jar, measuring cups, knife, cutting board

INGREDIENTS TO HAVE:

6 cups **spring mix salad greens**

¼ cup **olive oil**

2 tablespoons **balsamic vinegar**

2 tablespoons **honey mustard**

2 tablespoons **maple syrup**

1 cup chopped **pineapple**

½ cup **sunflower seeds**

½ cup **pumpkin seeds**

½ cup **dried cranberries**

The seeds, dried fruit, and amazing dressing on this salad will leave you heading back for seconds! Taking it on the go? Store the dressing separately and add when you are ready to eat.

1. **Prepare salad greens.** Wash and dry the mixed greens and put them into a large bowl.

2. **Make dressing.** Mix the oil, vinegar, honey mustard, and maple syrup together in a mason jar or glass container with a lid and shake well.

3. **Chop the pineapple.** Carefully peel and chop fresh pineapple until you have 2 cups. If using canned pineapple, drain out the liquid before chopping.

4. **Make the salad.** Toss the salad greens in the dressing and top with sunflower and pumpkin seeds, cranberries, and pineapple sprinkled on top.

THE GOOD STUFF

Why salad greens instead of lettuce? Because the darker the green, the more disease-fighting nutrients are inside.

CHICKPEA-STUFFED PEPPERS

DAIRY-FREE GLUTEN-FREE VEGETARIAN

PREP TIME
15 minutes

COOK TIME
50 minutes

MAKES
4
SERVINGS

TOOLS TO GATHER

baking stone/ baking dish, cutting board, food processor, knife, measuring cups, measuring spoons, mixing bowl, strainer

INGREDIENTS TO HAVE:

2 (15-ounce) cans **chickpeas**

1 cup **cashews**

3 tablespoons **avocado oil**

2 tablespoons **almond flour**

1 tablespoon **dried parsley**

1 **garlic clove**, peeled

2 **bell peppers**

¼ cup **tahini**

2 tablespoons **almond milk**

Juice of 1 **lemon**

2 tablespoons **water**

Whether whipped into a hummus or made into falafel (or something in between), chickpeas are always a treat. When you bake them in a pepper, you know the flavor and nutrition will be over the top.

1. **Preheat oven.** Set the oven to 400° F.

2. **Make the stuffing.** Open cans of chickpeas, then drain and rinse them. Combine chickpeas, cashews, oil, almond flour, parsley, and garlic in a food processor. Blend until you achieve a smooth consistency.

3. **Prepare peppers.** Wash and slice the bell peppers in half and remove the seeds. Fill each half evenly with the chickpea mixture. Place on a baking stone. Bake in the oven for 50 minutes, until the tops are golden brown.

4. **Make sauce.** Meanwhile, create a tahini sauce by combining tahini, almond milk, lemon juice, and water in the food processor. Pulse until smooth. Transfer into a small bowl or jar and set aside.

THE GOOD STUFF

Peppers are packed with vitamin C which helps keep cold viruses away and also helps keep our teeth and gums healthy. Maybe you could invite your dentist for supper and serve them this meal.

5. **Cool and add tahini.** Remove peppers from the oven. Let cool for 5 minutes then drizzle with tahini sauce.

BURRITO
SALAD BOWL

PAGE **92**

DINNER

✓ MEASURING
✓ STOVE

BURRITO SALAD BOWL

PREP TIME
10 minutes

COOK TIME
25 minutes

MAKES
6
SERVINGS

TOOLS TO GATHER

can opener, cutting board, frying pan, knife, measuring cups, measuring spoons, pot, strainer

INGREDIENTS TO HAVE:

2 cups **water**

1 cup **quinoa**

1 pound extra-lean **ground chicken**

2 tablespoons **taco seasoning**

2 **avocados**

2 **tomatoes**

4 ounces **cheese**

1 (15-ounce) can **black beans**

4 handfuls **baby spinach**

1 cup **salsa**

This is not an ordinary salad. It starts with a base of iron-rich spinach and has wonderfully filling and flavorful toppings. It is a true meal!

1. **Cook quinoa.** Place the water and quinoa in a small pot. 🖐 Bring to a boil over high heat. Once boiling, reduce heat to a simmer and cover. Let simmer for 12 minutes or until all water is absorbed. Remove from heat, fluff with a fork, and set aside.

2. **Cook chicken.** 🖐 Put the ground chicken in a nonstick frying pan and cook over medium heat. Stir every 3 to 4 minutes to prevent burning. Add 1 to 2 tablespoons of water if needed to keep the chicken moist. Once the chicken is cooked, stir in taco seasoning.

3. **Dice avocado and tomato.** 🖐 Dice the tomato. Cut avocado in half, remove the skin and pit, and dice the green flesh.

4. **Prepare cheese and beans.** 🖐 Grate 1 cup of shredded cheese. Open the can of beans, drain, and rinse the beans.

Cheese is an excellent source of calcium. Calcium is important for our bone length and density. And since you only have until you are 30 for your bones to get longer and stronger, you want to make sure to eat calcium every day (also found in milk, yogurt, broccoli, almonds, and fortified drinks).

5. **Assemble burrito bowls.** Place spinach into 4 bowls. This will mean 1 handful in each bowl. Then add other ingredients in a clockwise pattern in the following quantities: ½ cup cooked quinoa, ½ cup cooked ground chicken, ¼ cup diced avocado, ¼ cup diced tomato, ¼ cup black beans, ¼ cup salsa, ¼ cup shredded cheese.

EPIC CHICKEN WITH CARROT FRIES

GLUTEN-FREE   NUT-FREE

PREP TIME
20 minutes

COOK TIME
45 minutes

MAKES

6

SERVINGS

TOOLS TO GATHER

baking dish, baking stone, cutting board, knife, measuring cups, mixing bowl, vegetable peeler

INGREDIENTS TO HAVE:

12 medium **carrots**

2 tablespoons **avocado oil**

½ teaspoon **sea salt**

¼ cup **orange juice**

¼ cup **honey**

¼ cup **mustard**

6 boneless, skinless **chicken breasts**

1 **avocado**

½ cup **ranch dressing**

It's like chicken fingers and fries with WAY more nutrition. This recipe is great served on its own or with a side of brown rice.

1. **Preheat oven.** Set the oven to 375°F.

2. **Prepare vegetables.** Wash, peel, and slice carrots. Toss in avocado oil and salt in a mixing bowl and lay them on a baking stone or baking dish. Set aside.

3. **Make the sauce.** Mix together the orange juice, honey, and mustard.

4. **Prepare the chicken.** Place chicken breasts on a separate baking dish. Pour sauce evenly over top of the chicken breasts. Cover the pan in aluminum foil.

5. **Cook the chicken and carrots.** Place both pans on the middle rack of the oven for about 45 minutes. You will know the carrots are done when they are softened throughout. The chicken is done when juices run clear.

6. **Make the dip.** Peel and pit the avocado. Mash the green flesh in a small bowl using a fork. Mix in the ranch dressing. Serve the chicken with the dip on the side.

THE GOOD STUFF

Chicken is a wonderful source of iron. Iron is a really special nutrient because it helps our blood carry oxygen to our muscles and brain. If you don't have enough iron in your diet you may feel tired and weak. You may also get sick more often. So, I guess it's time to eat up that chicken.

SAVE-THE-DAY SALMON WITH BUTTERNUT SQUASH

DAIRY-FREE   GLUTEN-FREE   NUT-FREE

PREP TIME
15 minutes

COOK TIME
50 minutes

MAKES
6
SERVINGS

TOOLS TO GATHER

baking dishes, cutting board, knife, measuring cups, mixing bowl, peeler

INGREDIENTS TO HAVE:

¼ cup **maple syrup**

¼ cup **low-sodium soy sauce**

1 teaspoon **minced garlic**

½ teaspoon **minced ginger**

1 **butternut squash**

2 tablespoons **coconut sugar**

1 tablespoon **avocado oil**

6 (4-ounce) **salmon fillets**

This meal has a touch of sweetness to each nourishing bite. It is packed with protein, omega-3 fatty acids, iron, and beta carotene. So, your whole body will thank you every time you enjoy it. Try adding a splash of green with a side of steamed broccoli or snap peas.

1. **Preheat oven.** Set the oven to 400°F.

2. **Prepare sauce.** In a small bowl, mix together the maple syrup, soy sauce, garlic, and ginger.

3. **Prepare butternut squash.** Peel and cut the butternut squash into bite-size chunks. Place the squash in a baking dish and mix with the sugar and oil. Cover with aluminum foil and bake for 45 to 50 minutes, or until the squash pieces are softened throughout.

4. **Prepare salmon.** Place salmon fillets in a baking dish. Drizzle the sauce evenly over all the fillets. Cover with foil and place in the oven when the butternut squash has been in the oven for 25 minutes. Bake for 22 to 25 minutes, or until salmon flakes apart easily.

THE GOOD STUFF

Salmon is one of the best sources of omega-3 fatty acids. This is a key nutrient that the body cannot make—it has to come from food or a supplement. It is really important for brain growth and development. I guess that makes this the perfect supper the night before your next math test!

✓ KNIVES
✓ MEASURING
✓ STOVE
✓ OVEN

CREAMY CAULIFLOWER PASTA WITH PEAS

DAIRY-FREE   VEGETARIAN

PREP TIME
15 minutes

COOK TIME
1 hour

MAKES
6
SERVINGS

TOOLS TO GATHER

baking dish, cutting board, food processor, knife, large pot, measuring cups, measuring spoons, strainer

INGREDIENTS TO HAVE:

1 **cauliflower head**

1 **sweet onion**

2 tablespoons **avocado oil**

2 cups **whole-grain penne**

2 cups **cashews**

1 cup **coconut milk**

2 tablespoons **nutritional yeast**

2 **garlic cloves**, peeled

2 cups **frozen peas**

If you are a macaroni and cheese fan, this recipe is sure to excite you. The creaminess of blended cashews with the cheesy flavor of nutritional yeast can't be beat!

1. **Preheat oven.** Set the oven to 400°F.

2. **Roast onion and cauliflower.** 🖐 Wash and cut up the cauliflower and onion. Place in a glass baking dish and drizzle with avocado oil. Bake for 40 to 45 minutes until cauliflower is soft and slightly golden on the tips.

3. **Cook the pasta.** 🖐 While the vegetables are roasting, cook the penne pasta according to the directions on the package. Drain and set aside.

4. **Make the sauce.** Combine cashews, coconut milk, nutritional yeast, and garlic cloves in a food processor and blend on high until a smooth sauce has formed. Add roasted cauliflower and onions and blend again until smooth.

5. **Mix everything together.** Add the cream sauce and peas to the pot of pasta. Warm over medium heat until hot. Enjoy!

THE GOOD STUFF

Nutritional yeast is an amazing addition to dairy-free meals because it has a "cheesy" flavor. It also comes with vitamin B_{12}, which is important for keeping our energy levels up. Nutritional yeast can be used as a tasty topping for popcorn, broccoli, and corn on the cob.

✓ KNIVES
✓ MEASURING
✓ OVEN

SECRET IDENTITY PIZZA

NUT-FREE   VEGETARIAN

PREP TIME
10 minutes

COOK TIME
15 minutes

MAKES
4
SERVINGS

TOOLS TO GATHER

baking stone/ baking sheet, cutting board, knife, measuring cup, measuring spoon

INGREDIENTS TO HAVE:

6 **figs**

1 large handful **arugula**

1 (10- to 12-inch) **whole-grain pizza crust**

2 tablespoons **avocado oil**

½ cup crumbled **goat cheese**

1 tablespoon **honey**

Goodbye pepperoni and mozzarella, hello figs and goat cheese. This is not your ordinary pizza . . . this pizza has pizazz!

1. **Preheat oven.** Set the oven to 400°F.

2. **Prepare toppings.** Cut figs into small pieces. Wash arugula and dry well.

3. **Make pizza.** Place pizza shell on pizza stone or baking sheet and spread avocado oil on it. Add figs and goat cheese.

4. **Bake pizza.** Put the pizza into the oven for 15 minutes, or until the edges are slightly brown.

5. **Add final toppings.** Remove the pizza and add the arugula to the top then drizzle the honey and serve.

THE GOOD STUFF

Figs come from one of the oldest types of trees and are a great sweet source of prebiotics. Prebiotics provide food to probiotics. Probiotics are called "good bacteria" because they keep our intestines healthy, which keeps us healthy. For days when you aren't adding figs to pizza, you can add them to yogurt or oatmeal or just eat them on their own for a quick snack.

MANGO-TOFU SALAD

✓ KNIVES
✓ MEASURING
✓ STOVE

DAIRY-FREE   GLUTEN-FREE   NUT-FREE   VEGETARIAN

PREP TIME
15 minutes

COOK TIME
15 minutes

MAKES
6
SERVINGS

TOOLS TO GATHER

can opener, cutting board, knife, measuring cup, mixing bowl, pot, strainer, wooden or silicone spoon

INGREDIENTS TO HAVE:

1 cup **quinoa**

2 cups **water**

10 ounces **extra firm tofu**

2 **avocados**

2 **mangos**

2 **limes**

1 (15-ounce) can **chickpeas** drained and rinsed

¼ cup chopped **fresh cilantro**

Did you know we taste first with our eyes, then our mouths? Our eyes don't have taste buds, but the way a dish looks makes a difference in how excited we are to eat it.

1. **Make quinoa.** Combine the quinoa and water in a medium-size pot. Place over high heat and bring to a boil. Once boiling, reduce the heat to a simmer and cover with a lid. Simmer for 13 to 15 minutes or until the water is absorbed. Remove lid and fluff with a fork.

2. **Prepare other ingredients.** Cut the tofu into 1-by-1-inch pieces and set aside. Peel and dice the avocados and mangos and set aside. Cut the limes into quarters and squeeze the juice into small bowl. Open can of chickpeas, then drain and rinse them.

3. **Make the salad.** In a large bowl, combine the quinoa, chickpeas, tofu, avocado, mango, lime juice, and cilantro. Mix and serve.

THE GOOD STUFF

Tofu offers phytochemicals that protect against some forms of cancer. It is always wonderful when food tastes good, fills us up, and protects against disease.

MIGHTY TURKEY CHILI

DAIRY-FREE   GLUTEN-FREE   NUT-FREE

PREP TIME
20 minutes

COOK TIME
1 hour

MAKES
8
SERVINGS

TOOLS TO GATHER

can opener, cutting board, knife, measuring cups, measuring spoons, pot, strainer

INGREDIENTS TO HAVE:

1 **bell pepper**

1 **onion**

1 **garlic clove**

1 (15-ounce) can **white kidney beans**

1 (15-ounce) can **red kidney beans**

2 pounds **lean ground turkey**

1 (28-ounce) can **diced tomatoes**

1 tablespoon **maple syrup**

1 teaspoon **chili powder**

1 teaspoon **turmeric**

This hearty meal is packed with protein, fiber, and sickness-fighting antioxidants. It is a great one to make ahead and enjoy on a busy evening between school and extracurriculars. Try serving it with your favorite crusty bread or crackers and a green salad.

1. **Prepare vegetables.** Wash the bell pepper, remove the core, and dice the remainder. Peel and dice the onion and garlic clove. Drain and rinse the red and white kidney beans.

2. **Cook the ground turkey.** Sauté the ground turkey in a pot on medium heat. Use a spoonful of water in the pan as needed for additional moisture.

3. **Add other ingredients.** Once turkey is cooked through, add tomatoes and their juices, beans, onion, bell pepper, maple syrup, chili powder, and turmeric.

TO BE CONTINUED . . .

FLAVOR BOOST

Try topping chili with a spoonful of Greek yogurt or sour cream, shredded cheese, and diced tomatoes.

4. **Simmer for the best flavor.** Let simmer on low heat setting for 30 to 60 minutes, until the flavors combine.

THE GOOD STUFF

Beans are an incredible source of fiber. Fiber helps to move waste through us, but it also helps to clean up the "bad" cholesterol in our body which leads to better heart health. Yay for beans!

MEATLOAF MUFFINS WITH MASHED POTATO "ICING"

DAIRY-FREE   GLUTEN FREE   NUT-FREE

PREP TIME
25 minutes

COOK TIME
25 minutes

MAKES
6
SERVINGS

TOOLS TO GATHER

knife, cutting board, measuring cups, measuring spoons, medium pot, mixing bowl, muffin tin

INGREDIENTS TO HAVE:

FOR THE MEATLOAF

1 **onion**

2 pounds **lean ground beef**

2 tablespoons **Dijon mustard**

1 teaspoon **ground sage**

1 teaspoon minced **garlic**

FOR THE ICING

5 medium **potatoes**

½ cup **coconut milk**

¼ cup **tomato sauce**

Cupcakes for supper? Yes please! This yummy dinner has the fun look of cupcakes with the nutrition of a traditional meal. These are perfect for your sister's birthday or any ordinary Wednesday!

TO MAKE THE MEATLOAF

1. **Preheat oven.** Set the oven to 350° F.

2. **Dice onion.** Peel and cut the onion into small pieces.

3. **Mix ingredients together.** In a mixing bowl, combine the beef, onion, mustard, sage, and garlic until well combined.

4. **Bake the muffins.** Grease the cups of a 12-cup muffin tin and divide mixture evenly into the cups. Bake for 20 to 25 minutes or until cooked through and there is no pink in the center of a muffin cut open.

TO BE CONTINUED . . .

SWAP IT

You can also make this recipe with ground chicken or turkey.

THE GOOD STUFF

Garlic and onions have an antioxidant called "allicin." Allicin helps the body fight off viruses and bacteria. To get the greatest benefit, try enjoying a little bit of raw onion or garlic each day. Adding it to cooked dishes is a great way to enjoy it too.

TO MAKE THE ICING

1. **Make the mashed potato icing.** 👋 While the meatloaf is cooking, cut the potatoes into medium-size pieces and place them in a pot on the stove with 2 to 3 cups of water. Bring the water to a boil and then cook the potatoes on medium until softened. This will take about 15 minutes. Once they are cooked, drain the water, mash potatoes down with a fork, and add the coconut milk. Stir until the potatoes are smooth.

2. **Assemble the meatloaf muffins.** When the meatloaf muffins are ready, top each one with about a teaspoon of tomato sauce. Then, top it with the potato mash and spread evenly using the back of a spoon.

SPINACH-LENTIL CURRY

✓ MEASURING
✓ STOVE

DAIRY-FREE   GLUTEN-FREE   NUT-FREE   VEGETARIAN

PREP TIME
15 minutes

COOK TIME
45 minutes

MAKES
4
SERVINGS

TOOLS TO GATHER

frying pan, measuring cups, measuring spoons, mixing bowl, pots

INGREDIENTS TO HAVE:

1 cup **lentils**

¾ cup **jasmine rice**

2 tablespoons **avocado oil**

2 tablespoons **curry powder**

1 tablespoon **garlic powder**

1 cup **low-sodium vegetable broth**

½ cup **coconut milk**

6 cups **baby spinach**

2 tablespoons **maple syrup**

Curry dishes hit the taste buds on our tongue that notice savory or "umami" flavors. This dish is as beautiful as it is flavorful, making it very fun to serve and eat.

1. **Prepare lentils and rice.** Cook the lentils and rice in separate pots according to the instructions on their packages.

2. **Prepare the paste.** In a small bowl, mix together the oil, curry powder, and garlic powder into a paste. Set aside.

3. **Make lentils.** Pour vegetable broth and cooked lentils into a frying pan. Place a lid on top and bring to a boil, then reduce heat to medium for 10 to 15 minutes, until all the liquid is absorbed.

4. **Add the curry.** Remove lid and add curry paste and coconut milk. Simmer on low for an additional 10 minutes. Scrape any browned bits off the bottom of the pan.

5. **Add the spinach.** Remove the lid again and gently add handfuls of spinach, stirring them in as you go.

TO BE CONTINUED . . .

FLAVOR BOOST

Try adding a spoonful of coconut milk yogurt and a few leaves of cilantro to the top of this dish to add a little cool fresh flavor.

6. **Serve it up.** Scoop the rice onto plates. Add the curry mixture on top. Then drizzle with maple syrup.

THE GOOD STUFF

This meal offers a source of iron, but it isn't quite the same as the iron in the chicken we talked about earlier. When iron comes from animal sources the body can use it easily. When iron comes from plants, the body isn't able to use it as easily. It is like a key that fits into a lock but won't turn. The cool thing is that vitamin C helps to turn the key! So, adding a source of vitamin C on the side of this meal such as bell peppers, tomatoes, or oranges would be a great way to get the most nutrition possible.

CHOCOLATE
ALMOND BUTTER
SMOOTHIE BOWL

PAGE 113

DESSERT

Powerful Pumpkin Pudding

Chocolate Almond Butter Smoothie Bowl

Gingerbread Bites

Strawberry Banana Freeze

Warm Pears with Yogurt and Cinnamon

Avocado and Pea Brownies

POWERFUL PUMPKIN PUDDING

DAIRY-FREE GLUTEN-FREE NUT-FREE VEGETARIAN

PREP TIME
10 minutes

COOK TIME
40 to 45 minutes

MAKES
10
SERVINGS

TOOLS TO GATHER

baking dish, measuring cups, measuring spoons, mixing bowl

INGREDIENTS TO HAVE:

1 (30-ounce) can **pure pumpkin pureé**

1 **egg**

½ cup **rolled oats**

½ cup **coconut sugar**

2 teaspoons **cinnamon**

1 teaspoon **vanilla extract**

FLAVOR BOOST

For extra crunch, try adding pumpkin seeds to this recipe before you bake it.

If you like pumpkin pie, you are going to LOVE this pumpkin pudding. It's sweet and savory and can be enjoyed warm or cold.

1. **Preheat oven.** Set the oven to 375°F.

2. **Blend ingredients.** Add the pumpkin, egg, oats, coconut sugar, cinnamon, and vanilla to a food processor and blend until smooth.

3. **Bake pudding.** Grease an 8-by-8-inch baking dish, pour the batter into it, and bake for 45 minutes, or until a toothpick inserted into its center comes out clean.

THE GOOD STUFF

Pumpkins are a wonderful source of beta carotene. We talked about beta carotene in chapter 3 and how it can be converted to vitamin A for the body. But it is also an "anti-oxidant." This is a big word that means "fights against cell damage." How cool is it that you can enjoy a delicious dessert and fight off sickness at the same time?

CHOCOLATE ALMOND BUTTER SMOOTHIE BOWL

DAIRY-FREE GLUTEN-FREE VEGETARIAN

PREP TIME
5 minutes

MAKES
4
SERVINGS

TOOLS TO GATHER

blender, measuring cups, measuring spoons

INGREDIENTS TO HAVE:

2 **bananas**, fresh or frozen

2 cups **coconut milk**

1 cup frozen **cauliflower**

¼ cup **cocoa powder**

¼ cup **almond butter**

4 pitted **dates**

2 tablespoons **chia seeds**

½ cup **raspberries**

½ cup **granola**

This sweet and nutritious smoothie bowl is perfect for those times when you crave the smooth texture and sweet taste of ice cream but want to nourish your body. Craving a milkshake instead? Just add a little more milk and throw a straw in it.

1. **Blend ingredients.** Peel the bananas, then combine the bananas, coconut milk, cauliflower, cocoa powder, almond butter, dates, and chia seeds in a blender and blend until smooth.

2. **Pour smoothie into bowls.** Top with raspberries and granola. Serve and enjoy.

THE GOOD STUFF

Don't be fooled . . . chia seeds may be tiny, but they offer a powerhouse of protein. Chia seeds are unique in that they are one of a few plant-based protein sources that have everything the body needs to make a complete protein. In addition to this recipe, you can also sprinkle them on a bowl of oatmeal or yogurt.

✓ MEASURING
✓ OVEN

GINGERBREAD BITES

DAIRY-FREE   NUT-FREE   VEGETARIAN

PREP TIME
20 minutes

COOK TIME
12 to 15 minutes

MAKES
12
SERVINGS

TOOLS TO GATHER

baking sheet, measuring cups, measuring spoons, mixing bowl

INGREDIENTS TO HAVE:

¼ cup **coconut oil**

1 cup **whole-wheat flour**

½ cup unbleached **all-purpose flour**

1 teaspoon **baking powder**

1 teaspoon **ground ginger**

1 teaspoon **cinnamon**

1 **egg**

¼ cup **molasses**

¼ cup **maple syrup**

1 teaspoon **vanilla extract**

Who says gingerbread is only for the holiday season? These delicious bite-size cookies are a perfect addition to any lunch or supper year-round. Or maybe you would enjoy them with a glass of milk after school.

1. **Preheat oven.** Set the oven to 350° F.

2. **Prepare coconut oil.** In a small bowl, melt the coconut oil in the microwave. Set aside.

3. **Mix dry ingredients.** Combine the flours, baking powder, ginger, and cinnamon in a mixing bowl. Mix well using a fork to break up any clumps.

4. **Add wet ingredients.** Add in the coconut oil, egg, molasses, maple syrup, and vanilla. Mix again until blended well.

5. **Prepare the bites.** Roll the dough into balls about 2 tablespoons in size and place on a greased baking sheet. Gently flatten each ball with the palm of your hand.

6. **Bake the bites.** Bake for 12 to 15 minutes, until they are golden on the outside but still soft on the inside. Remove from oven and let cool completely. Enjoy!

THE GOOD STUFF

Did you know that ginger is helpful for calming an upset stomach? A ginger tea would be more soothing than a cookie (most likely), but you never know . . . try a cookie if you aren't feeling 100 percent, and it just might work.

STRAWBERRY BANANA FREEZE

DAIRY-FREE   GLUTEN-FREE   NUT-FREE   VEGETARIAN

PREP TIME
5 minutes

MAKES
4
SERVINGS

TOOLS TO GATHER

blender/food processor, measuring cups, measuring spoons

INGREDIENTS TO HAVE:

2 cups sliced frozen **bananas**

2 cups frozen **strawberries**

½ cup **coconut milk**

1 tablespoon **maple syrup**

SWAP IT

You can change up the flavors in this recipe by exchanging the strawberries for other fruit like frozen pineapple, mango, raspberries, or even coconut.

This is an amazing dessert that tastes like ice cream, but is packed with vitamin C, potassium, and more that will keep your body healthy and strong.

1. **Blend ingredients.** Combine the bananas, strawberries, coconut milk, and maple syrup in a blender or food processor and blend. Scrape down the sides every once in a while, and blend until smooth, 3 to 5 minutes.

2. **Scoop into a bowl.** You can enjoy this right away, or for a firmer ice cream, place in an airtight, freezer-safe container and freeze for at least 1 hour before scooping.

THE GOOD STUFF

Bananas are a great source of a mineral called "potassium." Potassium has a really cool role in keeping our blood vessels healthy. This means that is helps prevent blockages that can stop blood from getting to the heart and brain.

WARM PEARS WITH YOGURT AND CINNAMON

✓ KNIVES
✓ MEASURING
✓ OVEN

GLUTEN-FREE   NUT-FREE   VEGETARIAN

PREP TIME
10 minutes

COOK TIME
15 minutes

MAKES
4
SERVINGS

TOOLS TO GATHER

baking dish, cutting board, knife, measuring cup, measuring spoon

INGREDIENTS TO HAVE:

4 **pears**

1 tablespoon **ground cinnamon**

1 cup **vanilla yogurt**

It's like pear pie without the crust! Roasted pears are delicious anytime of the day and make a perfect sweet treat to end a meal.

1. **Preheat oven.** Set the oven to 375°F.

2. **Prepare pears.** Cut the pears in half and lay them in a glass baking dish with the cut sides up. Sprinkle cinnamon on top.

3. **Bake pears.** Cover the dish with foil and bake at for 12 to 15 minutes, until softened.

4. **Serve with yogurt.**

THE GOOD STUFF Ground cinnamon is one of the most common spices used in baking. Not only does it add a beautiful sweet and savory flavor, but it also helps to keep your body feeling balanced and your heart healthy.

AVOCADO AND PEA BROWNIES

DAIRY-FREE   NUT-FREE   VEGETARIAN

PREP TIME
15 minutes

COOK TIME
20 minutes

MAKES
12
SERVINGS

TOOLS TO GATHER

baking dish, food processor/blender, measuring cups, measuring spoons, knife, cutting board

INGREDIENTS TO HAVE:

1 **avocado**

2 **eggs**

½ cup **frozen peas**, thawed

½ cup **coconut sugar**

3 tablespoons **avocado oil**

½ teaspoon **vanilla extract**

½ cup **whole-wheat flour**

½ cup **cocoa powder**

1 teaspoon **baking soda**

⅓ cup **dark chocolate chips**

Enjoying sweet bites can be part of a healthy life. It's great to think of ways to add a boost of nutrition to these bites too. The avocado and peas in this recipe give a boost of healthy fats and protein to feed the brain and body while you feed your sweet craving.

1. **Preheat oven.** Set the oven to 350°F.

2. **Blend wet ingredients.** Halve, peel, and remove the pit from the avocado. Combine the avocado, eggs, peas, coconut sugar, avocado oil, and vanilla in a food processor or blender and mix well until combined.

3. **Add dry ingredients.** Add flour, cocoa powder, and baking soda. Process again until combined. Stir in the chocolate chips, reserving about 2 tablespoons to place on top.

4. **Bake brownies.** Transfer the batter to an 8-by-8-inch baking dish. Smooth the top down and sprinkle the remaining chocolate chips on top. Bake for 18 to 20 minutes, until a toothpick inserted in the center comes out clean.

TO BE CONTINUED . . .

SWAP IT

Do you want a gluten-free dessert? Just swap the whole-wheat flour with almond flour or coconut flour.

5. **Let cool.** Remove from the oven and let cool before cutting into bites.

THE GOOD STUFF

Did you know that the peas and flour in this recipe work together to give the body protein? Peas are one of a few vegetables that offer a source of protein, but they are missing one amino acid. The flour has that missing amino acid. What a team!

Nutritional Stats (per serving)

	Calories	Fat (g)	Sat. Fat (g)
COOKING SKILLS			
PEACHES AND CREAM SMOOTHIE	220	6	2.5
RAINBOW SALAD	140	0.5	0
OUT-OF-THIS-WORLD OATMEAL PANCAKES	380	6	1.5
PEANUT BUTTER PUMPKIN LOAF	220	15	2.5
BREAKFAST			
CAPED CRUSADER OVERNIGHT OATS	280	9	2
TROPICAL GREEN SMOOTHIE	140	3.5	3.5
MIGHTY MORNING MUFFINS	210	7	1
WAKE-UP BREAKFAST CUPS	330	17	5
LET'S ROLL! BANANA SUSHI	560	28	3.5
AMAZING AVOCADO TOAST	280	18	3.5
BEST BREAKFAST PIZZA	520	33	11
BLUEBERRY BLAST BREAKFAST CAKE	180	8	1
MARVELOUS MINI EGG CUPS	140	10	4.5
RADICAL RASPBERRY CHIA PUDDING	270	18	9
SNACKS			
AWESOME APPLE NACHOS	230	7	1

Sodium (mg)	Carbs (g)	Fiber (g)	Sugar (g)	Protein (g)
120	35	2	32	10
0	36	5	28	2
140	66	8	15	15
55	17	9	9	7
30	45	6	15	8
35	26	3	16	2
100	33	3	15	6
5	40	6	16	8
360	71	4	19	16
230	26	7	5	9
790	34	5	6	28
50	23	3	8	5
170	3	0	2	10
50	27	11	10	8
20	42	5	34	5

	Calories	Fat (g)	Sat. Fat (g)
SNACKS (CONTINUED)			
ON-THE-GO TRAIL MIX	250	16	4
ZIPPY ZUCCHINI CHOCOLATE CHIP COOKIES	360	18	7
STONE FRUIT SALAD	80	0	<1
KALE CHIPS FOR CHAMPS	170	8	1
QUINOA ENERGY BITES	420	19	3
CRISPY CRUNCHY CHICKPEAS	130	6	0.5
MELON SUPER SLUSHY	160	2	1.5
ALMOND BUTTER AND DATE BOATS	400	19	2
PROTEIN-PACKED BROWNIES	370	26	7
LUNCH			
TURBO TURKEY WRAP	290	9	2
BA-BAM! BAGEL PIZZA	450	19	9
CHEESY CARROT QUESADILLAS	440	23	13
SPEEDY SALMON BITES	220	15	2.5
EGGY BOATS	90	7	1
MAGIC TUNA MELTS	280	9	4.5
CREAMY TOMATO SOUP	150	5	1.5
SWEET POTATO PANCAKES	380	17	9
GREEK SALAD	300	21	7

Sodium (mg)	Carbs (g)	Fiber (g)	Sugar (g)	Protein (g)
60	28	3	14	7
68	45	5	19	13
88	20	2	17	1
90	21	5	5	8
10	55	5	25	14
120	16	0	6	3
55	32	2	28	6
6	61	6	49	6
25	26	3	11	16
510	37	1	3	26
1,780	38	5	5	32
770	40	2	5	21
150	6	1	3	16
75	7	3	2	3
530	24	0	2	27
340	25	5	16	4
210	41	4	18	15
590	25	6	15	9

	Calories	Fat (g)	Sat. Fat (g)
LUNCH (CONTINUED)			
TRAIL MIX SALAD	440	28	3.5
CHICKPEA-STUFFED PEPPERS	580	37	5
DINNER			
BURRITO SALAD BOWL	430	24	8
EPIC CHICKEN WITH CARROT FRIES	470	18	2.5
SAVE-THE-DAY SALMON WITH BUTTERNUT SQUASH	410	18	4
CREAMY CAULIFLOWER PASTA WITH PEAS	510	25	5
SECRET IDENTITY PIZZA	360	16	6
MANGO-TOFU SALAD	360	12	1.5
MIGHTY TURKEY CHILI	380	11	3.5
MEATLOAF MUFFINS WITH MASHED POTATO "ICING"	310	8	3.5
SPINACH-LENTIL CURRY	310	8	1.5
DESSERT			
POWERFUL PUMPKIN PUDDING	70	1	0
CHOCOLATE ALMOND BUTTER SMOOTHIE BOWL	360	17	4.5
GINGERBREAD BITES	140	5	4
STRAWBERRY BANANA FREEZE	100	1	0.5
WARM PEARS WITH YOGURT AND CINNAMON	170	2	1
AVOCADO AND PEA BROWNIES	150	9	3

Sodium (mg)	Carbs (g)	Fiber (g)	Sugar (g)	Protein (g)
90	40	7	28	11
340	49	4	10	19
670	30	5	3	30
710	42	8	25	37
460	38	4	15	26
85	60	7	10	19
440	52	2	20	12
210	53	7	14	14
450	32	3	9	40
130	31	3	4	26
80	50	4	8	9
15	13	1	6	3
50	53	9	30	8
40	21	1	8	3
10	25	2	14	1
35	35	1	25	3
125	17	3	8	4

Measurement Conversions

Volume Equivalents (Liquid)

US STANDARD	US STANDARD (OUNCES)	METRIC (APPROXIMATE)
2 tablespoons	1 fl. oz.	30 mL
¼ cup	2 fl. oz.	60 mL
½ cup	4 fl. oz.	120 mL
1 cup	8 fl. oz.	240 mL
1½ cups	12 fl. oz.	355 mL
2 cups or 1 pint	16 fl. oz.	475 mL
4 cups or 1 quart	32 fl. oz.	1 L
1 gallon	128 fl. oz.	4 L

Oven Temperatures

FAHRENHEIT (F)	CELSIUS (C) (APPROXIMATE)
250°F	120°C
300°F	150°C
325°F	165°C
350°F	180°C
375°F	190°C
400°F	200°C
425°F	220°C
450°F	230°C

Volume Equivalents (Dry)

US STANDARD	METRIC (APPROXIMATE)
⅛ teaspoon	0.5 mL
¼ teaspoon	1 mL
½ teaspoon	2 mL
¾ teaspoon	4 mL
1 teaspoon	5 mL
1 tablespoon	15 mL
¼ cup	59 mL
⅓ cup	79 mL
½ cup	118 mL
⅔ cup	156 mL
¾ cup	177 mL
1 cup	235 mL
2 cups or 1 pint	475 mL
3 cups	700 mL
4 cups or 1 quart	1 L

Weight Equivalents

US STANDARD	METRIC (APPROXIMATE)
½ ounce	15 g
1 ounce	30 g
2 ounces	60 g
4 ounces	115 g
8 ounces	225 g
12 ounces	340 g
16 ounces or 1 pound	455 g

Index

About the Author

NOELLE MARTIN, MScFN, RD is a registered dietitian with a master of science in foods and nutrition. She is also a mom of three boys. Noelle has a passion for helping people in the areas of maternal and pediatric nutrition, sports nutrition, and food allergies or intolerances. In addition to her work in recipe development and writing, Noelle is a university instructor and enjoys counseling and running workshops. Her blogs, *Nourished Beginnings* and *Motherhood and Meals*, are dedicated to educating and inspiring moms to make healthy choices for themselves and their families.

Printed in the USA
CPSIA information can be obtained
at www.ICGtesting.com
CBHW081247200224
4497CB00002B/13

9 781641 529006